DACIA

T0371101

DACIA

AN OUTLINE
OF THE EARLY CIVILIZATIONS OF
THE CARPATHO-DANUBIAN
COUNTRIES

BY

VASILE PÂRVAN

CAMBRIDGE
AT THE UNIVERSITY PRESS
1928

CAMBRIDGE
UNIVERSITY PRESS

32 Avenue of the Americas, New York NY 10013-2473, USA

Cambridge University Press is part of the University of Cambridge.

It furthers the University's mission by disseminating knowledge in the pursuit of education, learning and research at the highest international levels of excellence.

www.cambridge.org
Information on this title: www.cambridge.org/9781107486676

© Cambridge University Press 1928

This publication is in copyright. Subject to statutory exception and to the provisions of relevant collective licensing agreements, no reproduction of any part may take place without the written permission of Cambridge University Press.

First published 1928
First paperback edition 2015

A catalogue record for this publication is available from the British Library

ISBN 978-1-107-48667-6 Paperback

Cambridge University Press has no responsibility for the persistence or accuracy of URLs for external or third-party internet websites referred to in this publication, and does not guarantee that any content on such websites is, or will remain, accurate or appropriate.

CONTENTS

TRANSLATORS' PREFACE

In March, 1926, Professor Pârvan gave a short course of lectures at Cambridge on the Early Civilizations of the Carpathian and Lower Danubian Countries. He came at the invitation of the Special Board for Classics and stayed as the guest of St John's College. It was felt that some permanent memorial of his visit might be of considerable interest to a wider public and the Cambridge University Press kindly undertook the publication of this book, which embodies the substance of his lectures. The first draft of the text was dictated by the author when he was already suffering from the illness which was soon to prove fatal, and could not be revised by him. It has been translated into English as a slight token of esteem to the memory of a great scholar and a charming friend.

Born in a little Moldavian village in 1882, Vasile Pârvan sprang from the ranks of a people imbued with 'a strange instinct for its Latinity.' At the local lycée he acquired a sound grounding in Classics which served him in good stead when he went as a student, first to Bucarest and then to Germany. The dissertation which he presented

for his doctorate at Breslau in 1909—*Die Nation-
alität der Kaufleute im römischen Kaiserreiche*—
was at once recognized as an important contribution to scholarship. But the task which he made
his life work was the active prosecution of excavations in the rich but little explored regions of his
native land.

His energy was phenomenal. To a masterly
knowledge of earlier work undertaken by Roumanian, German and Magyar archaeologists in
this little known field, he added the firstfruits of
a whole series of excavations carried out, for over
fifteen years, either directly by himself or under
his supervision. As Professor at the University
of Bucarest and Director of the Roumanian
School at Rome (which owed its foundation in
no small measure to his own activity), he gathered
round him a whole school of young men to whom
he imparted something of his own insatiable
curiosity. Under his auspices, the results of their
research began to appear, in French, in the
annual periodical, *Dacia—Recherches et Découvertes archéologiques en Roumanie* which Pârvan
himself instituted in 1924. His plan of publishing
a comprehensive account of his own finds at
Istria layer by layer had unfortunately not proceeded farther, at the time of his death, than a
description of Istria IV, which appeared in the

Annals of the Roumanian Academy for 1916 and 1923.

His failing health made him concentrate more than ever on his work. As permanent secretary of the Roumanian Academy and as director of the *Cultura Nationala*, a publishing house with a high educational and artistic purpose to fulfil, he played a very important rôle in the intellectual life of his native land. His largest and most comprehensive contribution to archaeological studies —*Getica*—appeared in the year of his death. Here he attempted a synthesis of the early history of the Carpatho-Danubian countries down to the end of the Roman era, with ample documentation and a wealth of illustrations. Readers of this present volume who desire to examine further the material and evidence upon which the author's conclusions are based will find them fully treated in *Getica*.

It has seemed best to place the illustrations all together at the end of this book. References to the plates are indicated in the text by numerals in Clarendon type. The blocks themselves have been selected from *Getica* and have been kindly lent by the Roumanian Academy.

The translators wish to thank Professor Adcock, of King's College, Professor Minns, of Pembroke College, Mr J. M. de Navarro, of Trinity College,

and Mr C. T. Seltman, of Queens' College, for
their very great kindness in reading through the
proofs and making many valuable suggestions.
The map was drawn by M. Dionisie Pecuranu, of
the Muzeul Naţional de Antichitaţi at Bucarest,
on the basis of material supplied by two former
assistants of Professor Pârvan—Dr Ecaterina
Vulpe and Dr Radu Vulpe. To them, as to the
officials of the Cambridge University Press, the
translators cannot sufficiently express their
gratitude.

I. L. EVANS
M. P. CHARLESWORTH

St John's College
  Cambridge

PLATES

after p. 204

Map. Available for download from www.cambridge.org/9781107486676

Chapter I

CARPATHO-DANUBIANS AND VILLANOVANS

THE Danubian lands of Central Europe extend
from the Austrian Alps in the west to the
plateaux of Eastern Galicia and the steppe country
of the Dobruja in the east. From the beginnings
of proto-history in the Bronze Age down to the
end of the Middle Ages, when the Catholic kingdom of the Hungarians fell before the onslaught
of their near relatives the Ottoman Turks in 1526,
this region exhibits a whole series of forms of civilization of which the territorial basis, as it were,
was the high plateau land of Transylvania.

This great natural fortress is roughly in the
form of a square, with lofty mountains on every
side. It contains deposits of gold and silver, of
copper, of iron and of salt. From the earliest neolithic times, inhabitants of the plains of Moldavia
and South Russia, with their beautiful painted
pottery, no less than wanderers from the thickly
peopled plains of the Middle Danube and the high-
lands of Illyria, with their incised pottery, succeeded in overcoming all the obstacles of nature
and penetrated, from the east and from the west,
into this mountain fortress with its stores of gold.
Here they settled down together, creating by their

fusion a new civilization of their own. Its characteristics were mainly western, though with certain
marked traces of eastern influences.

In the Bronze Age the Carpathians were the
cradle of the virile and original civilization of what
is called the 'Hungaro-Roumanian Bronze Age',
with workmanship in bronze and gold which was
unique in Europe. In the first Iron Age two civilizations used this same Carpathian region as a
basis for expansion towards the west. First came
the Cimmerians, who only remained a short time
but brought with them a curious type of copper
work modelled on Caucasian originals. Next came
the Scythians, who remained for a very long
period, and introduced naturalistic designs of
Russo-Siberian type. Again, in the second Iron
Age, the original inhabitants of this region, which
we may now call by its proper name of Dacia,
drove back Iranian invaders eastwards and Celts
to the west, and founded the greatest barbarian
empire ever known in this part of Europe. The
Getic kingdom of Burebista included Bohemia
and Western Hungary, as well as Bessarabia and
Bulgaria, but the Transylvanian Carpathians remained the basis of its power. Even the Roman
conquests beyond the Eastern Alps and the
Adriatic were not complete until Dacia had
submitted. Later emperors withdrew behind the

Danube after little more than a century and a half of occupation, yet this Eastern Roman province, when it had once received the impress of Latin civilization, was the only one destined to succeed, in the face of the most severe trials, in maintaining its Roman characteristics right down to the present day.

A study of Danubian Europe in proto-historic and ancient times is therefore, above all, a consideration of the racial relationships, and an examination of the types of civilization which the Carpatho-Danubians of pre-Roman Dacia have to show us from about the end of the second millennium B.C., when these peoples begin to acquire names well-established in general history. It is not proposed, however, to advance hypotheses as to the nationality of the Carpatho-Danubians, but rather to let the facts speak for themselves. Let us begin, then, by describing this Danubian civilization as it was about the year 1000 B.C.

A careful archaeological study of the 'great period of the Hungaro-Roumanian Bronze Age' in Transylvania, as exemplified in innumerable hoards which were hidden first of all from Cimmerian invaders and then from the Iranians (that is to say, between 1000 and 700 B.C.), points to three important conclusions:

(1) The third period of the Carpatho-Danubian

Bronze Age is nothing more than a long preparation for the fourth period—the 'Golden Age'—
whose industrial products are a natural development from types of the preceding period. It really
makes no difference whether we take the middle
of the twelfth century B.C. (as Reinecke holds*),
or the end of the eleventh century B.C. (as we are
inclined to think), as the dividing line between
the two periods. In either case it is quite clear
that the latter half of the second millennium B.C.
was not disturbed by any invasion or devastation
such as would bring about important changes in
the ethnographic or cultural composition of the
Carpatho-Danubian countries.

(2) The bronze hoards of Bohemia and Western
Hungary exhibit the same cultural forms as we
find in the Carpathians. As in the days of Caesar,
there is direct continuity with the West.†

(8) The main characteristics of the industrial
products of Dacia are derived from the west
rather than from the east. In other words, there
is a more clearly marked connection with the west
of Central Europe, including Northern Italy, than
there is with Eastern and Southern Europe or
Asia Minor.

We know that the Iron Age began later in the

* *Archaelogiai Értesitő*, 1899, p. 225 sqq. and 316 sqq.
† Caesar, *De Bell. Gall.* VI, p. 24 sq.

Carpatho-Danubian region than in Noricum or in North-east Italy—that is to say, in those Veneto-Illyrian countries which controlled the overland route by which amber came from the Baltic as well as the maritime routes from the Adriatic to the Eastern Mediterranean. As in Western Gaul, the last period of the Bronze Age in the Carpathians lasted down to the end of the eighth century B.C. Yet the products of the Veneto-Illyrian lands in the second Iron Age and, more especially in the first half of this period, were by no means unknown to the Carpatho-Danubians. Just as the copper axe heads of Cimmerian type had long formed the object of a very active trade with Eastern Europe as far as the Ural Mountains and the Caucasus, so the beautiful bronze vases made in Italy at Ateste and Villanova, together with the helmets, breastplates, and greaves, which are technically the same type of product, spread through all the Carpatho-Danubian countries and even passed beyond the Dniester into Podolia. It is true that Cimmerian axe heads and Italic vases were imitated by the Dacians, and it is not always easy to distinguish between the foreign and the domestic product. The technique of making thin hammered sheets of bronze or gold, with repoussé or engraved ornamentation, was understood in Dacia as early as the third Bronze Age. Under

Veneto-Illyrian influence, however, this type of work developed very greatly, and the decorative patterns of the fourth Carpathian Bronze period approximate very closely to the models coming from the south-west.

Let us now outline the geographical distribution of Villanovan and Atestine products in Danubian Europe and then proceed to consider them from the stylistic point of view.

The districts in immediate proximity to Italy are not of any great interest for our present purpose. Styria, Carinthia, Carniola, Northern Dalmatia and even Western Hungary are a natural continuation of North Italic Venetia. It is therefore quite natural that we should find the products of the bronze-workers of Ateste and Villanova in these districts. What really establishes beyond dispute the essential unity of Danubian Europe is that similar products are discovered in very large numbers in Transylvania and in Galicia. These North Italic products are also found north of the Alps and even as far away as the Baltic coast and here they bear witness to that other great European unity, the Italo-Celtic, which penetrated far into Germanic territory. On the other hand, these products are virtually non-existent in the Balkan Peninsula, which, from this point of view, as from so many others, belongs

to a different world. Here Greek, or, to speak
more generally, Aegean influences are much more
important than they are in the Danubian lands.

The region which lies between the great Hungarian plain of the Middle Danube and the plateau of Eastern Galicia abounds in North Italic
products, which are usually found together with
native products belonging to the fourth period of
the Hungaro-Roumanian Bronze Age. Thanks to
the existence, side by side, of these two varieties—
the Carpatho-Danubian products on the one hand
and the Italo-Venetian on the other—we are able
to establish a fairly exact chronology. Reinecke,
in his classification of Hungaro-Roumanian
bronzes, also regards the fourth period of this Age
as contemporary with western influences of the
Italo-Hallstatt type, and distinguishes three
phases or sub-periods. The first, which corresponds
to the most ancient Villanovan period, would include the finds at Guşteriţa, Bundorf, Rus, Kasza-
púszta and Hajdú-Böszörmény. The second phase,
which appears to us difficult to separate from the
first, since in these deposits we find exactly the
same products of North Italic bronze-workers,
would include the finds at Brăduţ and at Kemecse.
The third, which, according to Reinecke, lasted
down to the middle of the ninth century but
which we think was much more recent and prob-

ably continued so late as the year 700 B.C., is
represented by the deposits at Şomărtin and,
above all, by the valuable find at Fizeşul Gherlii.
This last period would thus represent the tran-
sition towards the true Hallstatto-Carpathian
type—approximately contemporaneous with the
Scythian invasion—such as we find it at Aiud,
Gyoma and elsewhere.*

Of the metallic vases of North Italian origin—
cistae, situlae and hemispherical cauldrons—the
most widespread type found between the Middle
Danube and the Dniester is the small cauldron
with two movable handles and cruciform handle
mounts. These found their way into Galicia and
Podolia by way of trade. They were probably
taken over the Carpathians by the mountain
passes in what is now Slovakia. We know of five
examples from Uniz in Galicia, and seven at
Kungsowce on the Dniester, and of others in
Podolia. These cauldrons were the first North
Italic vessels to circulate through virtually the
whole of Central and Western Europe, from Gaul
to Galicia and from Styria to Denmark, towards
the end of the Bronze Age and the beginning of
the Iron Age. According to the proto-historic
chronology of the Alpine regions, this would be
between 1100 and 800 B.C. This conclusion also

* These are referred to in the next chapter, p. 54 sqq.

agrees perfectly with discoveries made in the Carpathian regions, since we find these cauldrons exclusively in the deposits of the fourth period, as we shall try to show later.

Such, then, are the geographic and chronological limits of Italic and Alpine infiltrations into the Carpatho-Danubian lands. We must now make a more detailed survey both of the location and of the style of the finds which establish the unity of cultural life in Danubian Europe during the Villanovan period. Among the most characteristic products of early Hallstatt industry is the *antennae* sword, an example of which was unearthed at Bundorf. This belongs, it is true, to the technique of the Bronze Age, but contains forms which already anticipate the first period of the Iron Age as known in the West. It was found side by side with two other swords belonging to the fourth period of the Carpatho-Danubian Bronze Age, and is the only specimen which has as yet been discovered to the east of the Middle Danube. The bronze-workers of the Carpathians never made *antennae* swords. This one must therefore have come through commercial channels. The period in which this type was manufactured in Switzerland, in the Alps and even in Italy was approximately the beginning of the first millennium B.C.

To this phase of the beginning of the fourth
period of the Carpatho-Danubian Bronze Age
belong the gold treasure and bronze deposits of
Brăduţ. Side by side with socketed axe heads,
sickles, sword fragments, and twenty-five gold
rings with transverse incisions, which may perhaps have served as money, we also find two specimens, of different size and decoration, of the
North Italic type of cauldron. Two other hemi-
spheric cauldrons have been found at Vécs, and
fragments of yet another at Alba-Iulia (the
ancient Apulum)[2]. We shall have more to say
later about other fragments discovered in the
large deposits at Guşteriţa, which date from the
beginning of the fourth period of the Carpatho-
Danubian Bronze Age. A fine cauldron of the
same type and in an excellent state of preservation
was found at Kántorjánosi in the county of Satmar[2]. The two districts which border on Satmar
and Bihor on the western side—the counties of
Szabolcs and Hajdú—are also very rich in these
cauldrons, which appear to be of Atestine and not
of Villanovan workmanship. The bronze merchant
who hid his treasure at Hajdú-Böszörmény was a
specialist in swords, and twenty-seven of these
survive. He also dealt, however, in the equally
valuable North Italic vases, of which the following
finds have been made: a fine *situla*[1], decorated

with solar symbols (the 'sunboat and swans' *motif*); a cauldron with two handles, of the well-known type[1]; a cup decorated with horizontal lines, dots and bosses, in repoussé, and characteristic of the fourth and fifth periods of the Bronze Age in Northern Europe[1]; and a bell-shaped helmet surmounted by a large knob, also in the Italic style, which is frequently met with in the Carpatho-Danubian regions. All these point to a period contemporaneous with that of the Villanovan finds at Benacci (between 1000 and 750 B.C.).

Cauldrons, whether whole or in fragments, have also been discovered at Máriapócs[2], Kis-Várda and Taktakenéz, together with a fine *situla*, found at Sényö, which is almost identical with that to which we have just referred. All these four places are situated in the county of Szabolcs. Similar cauldron handles of North Italic type have been discovered at Tobesdorf. In addition to numerous axe heads, the large bronze deposits of Fize-şul Gherlii[3] contain also certain fragments of cauldrons and very fine cups in a style which is North Italic, but a little more recent than that of the cauldrons from Brăduţ or Hajdú-Böszörmény.

These elements of the fourth Carpathian Bronze period, which are closely connected with the first Iron Age in the West do not consist merely of importations and of occasional imitations of

products brought from Northern Italy. The
workshops of Dacia themselves adopted new forms
inspired by western influences, whether Veneto-
Illyrian or Hallstatt, and produced original work
in the new style. The general tendency of the
period towards superficial ornament in repoussé
on thin metal plates rather than to more massive
effects, is also reflected in the Carpathian lands.
Something must therefore be said as to the
origin of this new style in bronze and in
gold in the countries to the east of the Middle
Danube.

Amongst the workshops of the fourth period of
the Bronze Áge, that at Spălnaca appears to have
occupied a leading place. Although not directly
influenced by authentic Hallstatt elements, this
workshop nevertheless anticipates the new tendencies. The fragments of bronze girdles—thin
plates ornamenting the broad leather girdles which
were well known in the West during the second
Hallstatt period—represent the well-known Venetic style of surface decoration, with chiselled
or engraved lines of purely geometric character.
This is not as yet, however, a direct western influence, but merely a parallelism on a similar
artistic basis.

Complete unity with the West shows itself very
soon afterwards. In the large deposit (or work-

shop) at Guşteriţa we find once more the characteristic swan heads[I] and a beautiful bronze girdle,
thirty-seven centimetres in diameter, which obviously belonged to a woman. This bears on it, in
chiselled work for the most part, the Mycenaean
pattern of a 'figure-of-eight' shield, solar discs
with four spokes, and, in the middle, a disc with
six spokes, zigzags and spirals. The master bronze-
worker of the Villanovan period, who executed
these decorations, was, however, merely repeat-
ing the patterns which we find on any Dipylon
vase in Athens—the solar disc, *svastica*, swan,
dots, zigzag lines and the draughtboard pattern.
Again, the representations of shields on other
Dipylon vases are identical with those of Guşteriţa
and are treated in the same decorative manner.
The Transylvanian Carpathians, far as they are
from Northern Italy and Attica, form part of one
and the same world. The first period of the North
Adriatic Iron Age witnessed in this region, at the
beginning of the fourth period of the Bronze Age,
the establishment of the very closest relations
with the South—with Italy on the one hand and
Greece on the other. Many of these southern
ideas, however, were not transmitted directly,
but were passed on by the Veneto-Illyrians of the
Northern Adriatic lands, who, without being very
original artists, were excellent men of business and

travellers, and worthy creators of a definite civilization in the first Iron Age.

We must look to the Danubian regions for further resemblances between these three civilizations. It is generally agreed that the spread of solar symbols towards the end of the Bronze Age and the beginning of the Iron Age throughout the whole of Western, Central and Northern Europe, was due to the artistic and religious influences of the South-eastern Alpine peoples (the Italo-Celto-Illyrians). The cult of the sun appears to have very ancient affinities in the Carpatho-Danubian region, for there are very many evidences of it in the remains that have come down to us from the fourth period of the Bronze Age. In addition to the examples we have already given above, it will be sufficient to mention a hemispherical bronze cauldron mounted on a four-wheeled votive car, the whole decorated with twelve swan heads[1], which was found not far from Orăştie,* and the votive bark with similar swan heads, found at Satmar, in order to see that the various bronze ornaments, so frequent in the fourth period of the Carpathian Bronze Age, are not a mere Veneto-Illyrian decorative influence, but arise from a deep artistic and religious feeling, indigenous in this region,

* Undset considered these to be of local workmanship. (See article by Hampel in *Arch. Értesitö*, 1895, p. 114.)

which was brought to new life by intimate contact with the Adriatic world.

We do not intend to enumerate here all the workshops, or, more accurately, all the bronze deposits which have been found to the east of the Middle Danube. It will suffice if we illustrate, by conclusive examples, the relations between the fourth period of the Carpathian Bronze Age, and the Earlier Hallstatt period in the West. From this point of view, however, we must mention the vases and golden discs from Biia, and the golden vases of Bihor, which are very closely connected with the finds of local bronze work of the fourth period; indeed these bosses in relief work, concentric circles and hemispherical profiles cannot be understood without reference to Veneto-Hallstatt forms. Similarly, the convex gold discs found at Otlaca[2], which are decorated with chiselled lines giving a naïve reproduction of geometric *motifs* or of animal patterns—birds, horses, or even of the human figure—cannot be separated from the analogous products of Illyro-Venetic art, even if our finds were actually manufactured in the district itself.

This powerful Villanovan and Atestine influence in the Carpathians was confirmed in a most remarkable manner by a sensational discovery made by Kovács, some ten years ago, at Târgul

Mureşului.* Side by side with funeral urns of an almost Villanovan biconical type which was very widespread throughout the first Carpatho-Danubian Iron Age and was almost certainly derived from the south-west, Kovács came across a clay vase, preserved intact, which reproduced very faithfully the outline of a metal vase of the proto-Etruscan type from Corneto (somewhere between 1000 and 900 B.C.)[4]. Although he imitated his metallic model, this Transylvanian potter did not neglect to decorate his work with oblique grooves on the body and horizontal grooves on the neck, in the ancient local style which had been in use since the Chalcolithic Age.

In addition, a discovery which is hardly less sensational was made at Donja Dolina, on the river Save, that is to say, on the principal route between Italy and Dacia. This shows us that Italic penetration in the Danubian countries was not limited to a mere export of Italic products through commercial channels, but that the North Italic industries themselves emigrated towards the Carpatho-Danubian region. In commenting on this discovery of a sandstone cast for *fibulae*, Truhelka† very properly makes the following remarks:

* Kovács in *Dolgozatok-Travaux*, Klausenburg, VI, 1915, p. 248 sqq.
† *Wissenschaftliche Mitteilungen aus Bosnien und Herzegowina*, IX (1904), p. 155.

The *fibulae* which were cast from this mould belong to a specifically Italic group and were never previously found in Bosnia....This entitles us to assume Italic influence, not merely as to importations, but also in the form of a direct immigration, for the presence of this foreign form of cast can only be explained on the supposition that an Italic bronze-worker had brought it over with the rest of his working equipment. In any case this one example is a much more conclusive proof of the close relations existing between Italy and the western Balkan countries than the whole series of Italic export goods which we have found up to the present.

If this type of *fibula* really belongs to the fourth period of the Italic Bronze Age—which we personally are inclined to doubt, so far, at least, as the period in which it was actually manufactured in Bosnia itself is concerned—we have here one of the clearest examples of the very distant period in which effective Italic penetration began to extend towards the east.

The Scythian invasion* interrupted these regular and intimate relations, but neither completely nor for all time. Even though *situlae* of Adriatic type have never actually been discovered in the Carpathian lands, we find, on the other hand, that *fibulae* of the Italic type had spread throughout Dacia.

A tomb at Oradea Mare has preserved for us a beautiful *fibula*, of the Certosa type, ornamented

* See Chapter II, infra, p. 36 sqq.

with a boar's head. A similar *fibula* was found at
Alba Iulia, and near by, at Marosportus, a small
navicella brooch and yet another of this type near
Deva. At Pişchi a special variety of the Hallstatt
bow-shaped *fibula* has been discovered and this
type is very widespread throughout the Carpatho-
Danubian and Balkan countries. The Hallstatt
centres of the western plain of Dacia at Pecica,
Otlaca and Gyoma on the right bank of the river
Mureş, and at Firighiaz, Carani, Beba-Veche and
Nagy-Gaj on the left bank, represent in a very
faithful manner the western or geometric style of
popular Carpatho-Danubian objects of adornment
developing on the old local basis in intimate connection with western types, but bearing no resemblance to Scythian forms.

The situation in the basin of the Târnava rivers
in Southern Transylvania is also very characteristic. At Sighişoara, which is virtually a Hallstatt
centre of the Alpine type, there have been found
bronze plates with broad flat rims like those from
Hallstatt itself. At Şoarş, again, two bronze helmets of the same North Italic type as at Hajdú-
Böszörmény or at Endröd have been discovered.
This is not surprising when we bear in mind the
large number of Italic products found in the Carpathians. Near-by, at Rodbav, a bow-shaped
fibula belonging to a rather more recent period

(600 to 500 B.C.) has been found, and yet another
of the Hallstatt type so common in these regions,
at Proştea-Mică. On the other hand, the bronze
vases at Şomărtin, which are of the same kind as
those of Fizeşul Gherlii,* bring us back once again
to Villanovan times.

The most characteristic feature, then, of these
early centuries of the first millennium B.C. in the
Carpatho-Danubian regions is their close cultural
connection with Italy and the Illyro-Celtic West.
This evolution is analogous to that in the Celto-
Germanic lands during the same period. Reinecke,
in considering the beginning of the Hallstatt Iron
Age and its relations with Italy, has also pointed
to the Villanovan elements, commencing with the
layer Benacci I (somewhere about the year 1000
B.C.), which appear at Sisak (Siscia), in Croatia,
Dálj, in Slavonia, Hajdú-Böszörmény and so on.
They spread to Prussia, to Transylvania and even
beyond the Carpathians for a considerable distance to the east and the south-east. These influences were due primarily to the very active
trade in Italic bronze vases. They were so common
that terra-cotta imitations of them were made
everywhere. As examples we may quote those
discovered at Kisköszeg or Târgul Mureşului[4].
On the other hand, L. Márton, in his detailed study

* Supra, p. 8.

of the *fibulae* found in the territory of pre-war
Hungary,* has pointed out the existence of a
whole series of close relationships between the
Carpatho-Danubian regions and Italy during the
Hallstatt period. The discoveries at Arcalia and at
Abos[5]prove that in North-eastern Transylvania,
as in Northern Slovakia, large chariots with two
bronze wheels were probably used for combats,
like those of Homeric days, rather than for ceremonial processions in honour of the sun god,
such as those which took place in Italy, in Gaul,
or in the Alpine region. In these areas the wheels
are of heavier form and smaller dimensions than
those found at Abos or at Arcalia, which have a
diameter of eighty centimetres. Déchelette is of
the opinion that these wheels, which are very
difficult to construct in bronze and in wood, must
also have been an industrial speciality of Veneto-
Illyria, and were spread through the rest of Europe
in the course of trade.† In addition to the copy
in pottery of a metal vase of the Corneto type,
found by Kovács at Târgul Mureşului[4], Hoernes
points to another Veneto-Dacian example of pure
jewelry work from Otlaca[2]. These gold discs, decorated with figures and chiselled geometric lines,

---

* *Arch. Értesitö*, 1918.
† Déchelette, *Manuel d'Archéologie Celtique*, i (Âge du
Bronze), p. 296.

are not of Venetic workmanship but are Central
European 'of degenerate Venetic type'.* In reality
we have here to do with a mixture of local patterns which, according to the suggestions and
comparisons made by L. Márton, appear to be
related to those of Mycenae.† The famous Hallstatt vases found at Scarbantia (Oedenburg), in
the Burgenland (now Austria), have their counterpart in the analogous urns found at Sfântu
Gheorghe, in Eastern Transylvania. Nothing
could be more natural, since *situlae* of Italian
origin spread to Denmark as well as to Transylvania. These relations led to an enormous diffusion
of certain decorative patterns, such as the concentric spiral. We find metal *fibulae* with double
or quadruple spirals in both Italic and Carpathian
tombs. This type of ornament is typical of the
Southern Hallstatt complex—Italy, Istria, Hungary, Roumania, with extensions to Southern
Italy and Greece. On the Villanovan type of pottery in Central Italy, on the other hand, we find
spectacle-spirals as the only circular decorative
pattern, in the midst of a profusion of straight
lines and angular incisions. The decorative pattern of the crescent (*ansae lunatae, cornutae*), which

* Hoernes-Menghin, *Urgeschichte der bildenden Kunst,*
p. 549 sqq.
† *Arch. Értesítö,* 1909, p. 405 sqq.

is so frequent on the Hallstatt vase handles of the
Western Balkans is quite as common in Italy as
in Dacia. We find analogies to the high-standing
pedestal dish, with broad, everted rim (which may
be considered as a classical product of the second
Iron Age in Dacia) in Italy and in the Hallstatt
Alps. The triangular holes on the feet of vases of
this type which have been found in Dacia, as, for
example, at Crăsani,* are also found in the same
form in Italy. Moreover, certain decorative varia-
tions like that of the triangle with its base itself
a re-entrant angle, are identical on a vase base
from Vulci (of the eighth century B.C.†) to quote
but one example, and on the bronze bells of Gyöngyös in Northern Hungary. The stones ornamented with spirals found at Nesactium, in
modern Istria (from the second Hallstatt period)
find their counterpart, also of a sacred character,
in the votive plaque at Sighişoara[4], though the
latter may be of slightly more recent date. The
Bolognese bronze bits of the Benacci I period
are similar to those of the same date which belong
to the fourth period of the Carpathian Bronze
Age. An ithyphallic statuette found at Mária-
Család in Western Slovakia is identical, both as

* In point of fact, these are very similar to the Scythian
bronze pole-tops at Bucarest and Ghernesig; cf. p. 45 and pl. 8.
† D. R. MacIver, *Villanovans and early Etruscans* (1924),
p. 175 (pl. 83–86).

to workmanship and form, with Italic statuettes
of the same type, from which Hoernes concludes
that it must be of Italic origin. The ornaments
discovered in the district of Tolna, in South-
western Hungary, on the other hand, are apparently nothing more than flimsy and not very skil-
ful imitations of Etruscan models.* In a similar
connection Reinecke points out that the *situla*
found at Kuffarn in Lower Austria belongs to the
same family of industrial products as the Arnoaldi
situla from Bologna.† So too, the clay bottle
found at Matzhausen in the Upper Palatinate‡
was not influenced by similar Rhodian or Corinthian vases, but had for its model an Italic *situla*
with an animal frieze, as is true, for that matter,
of the scabbard found at Hallstatt or the numerous *fibulae* of the Certosa type which have been
found throughout Central and South-eastern
Europe. Even the Etruscan products in Bucchero
ware were imitated in the countries north of the
Alps at a fairly recent date (say the fourth century or even later).

Naturally the main centre of the native civiliza-

* This is Hadaczek's suggestion. See *Röm. Mitt.* xxi (1906),
p. 387 sqq.
    † Reinecke, 'Zur Kenntniss der La Tène Denkmäler, etc.',
Mainzer Festschrift (1902), p. 76 sqq.
    ‡ Lindenschmit, *Altertümer unserer heidnischen Vorzeit*, v,
p. 282, fig. 2.

tion of South-eastern Europe in the heyday of
the Iron Age is to be found in the South-eastern
zone of Hallstatt culture on the shores of the
Adriatic. It is only here that we find stone sculpture work, in a semicircle, as it were, around the
northern gulf of this sea. As examples we may
cite those at Novilara near Pesaro, at Bologna,
at Este in Venetia, at Nesactium in the province
of Istria and at Ripač, near Bihać, in North-
eastern Bosnia. It is in this region that we see the
strongholds, called *castellieri*, constructed in accordance with a system of south-eastern origin
which, though not megalithic and still less in *opus
quadratum*, were nevertheless of regular construction and very strong, with walls several metres
high. Discoveries have shown that life had begun
there as early as the Neolithic Age. The bronze
arms and the pottery 'prove that civilization not
only continued down to the Bronze Age, but
actually reached its highest point in the Iron Age.
This conclusion is confirmed, from another point
of view, by the crematoria, which are sometimes
situated in immediate proximity to the *castellieri*'.*

In spite of the differences brought about in
the Bronze Age between the west of the Balkan
Peninsula, Western Hungary and the Thracian

* See A. Della Seta, *Italia antica*, p. 61 sqq.

regions of Carpatho-Danubia, the Iron Age thus
re-established the unity of Italo-Danubian civilization from Liguria and Apulia, in the West, as
far as the Northern Carpathians, Moldavia, and
even the Eastern Ukraine, in the East. The principal causes of this were the following: in the first
place, the extraordinary industrial and commercial
development of North-east Italy, with its mag-
nificent artistic bronze work; secondly, the analogous phenomenon of the iron-working region of
the Tirol, with a bronze industry almost as important as that in iron, which was its particular
speciality; and finally, the re-establishment, in
a form even more active than in the Bronze Age,
of the trade in amber, which now came not from
Jutland, but from East Prussia.

Upon their arrival on the Middle Danube, about
the year 700 B.C., the Scythians found a very
characteristic local civilization, impregnated, in
its turn, by Italic and Veneto-Illyrian elements,
which they shook to its very foundations. What
was this civilization, and to what people did it
belong?

The last period of the Carpathian Bronze Age,
which is a natural and peaceful development from
the third local period, does not finish until after
the Iranian penetration into these lands. Some
examples of late bronze work are still to be found

side by side with 'Scythian' objects. There was therefore a constant development of civilization in these regions, at any rate from the year 1400 B.C. onwards. We cannot say with certainty whether this period of peace, which was characterized by stable cultural relations and very probably by stable ethnographic conditions also, actually began as far back as the second period of the Carpatho-Danubian Bronze Age. This must remain an open question, and, for our present purpose, the point is of no direct interest.

A study of the distribution and types of the treasures hidden from the invaders enables us to establish a series of facts concerning the history and the civilization of the Carpatho-Danubian regions, from 1400 to 700 B.C., which may be summarized very briefly in the following manner.

The social and political life of the natives of the immense region lying between Bohemia and the Ukraine, and Dalmatia and Bulgaria, offers a series of phenomena very similar to those of the Achaeo-Mycenaean 'mediaeval' period. Our experience on the actual sites and in the archaeological atmosphere of the period has led us to the conclusion that the *Iliad* and the *Odyssey* may well serve, for the future, to illustrate many aspects of the proto-history of the natives of the Carpathians. Here are some of the characteristic features. Bronze, like gold, is scarce and dear. It is not used so much for tools as for arms and ornaments. It is rare in the sites of the period, which is a reason for concluding that it was not much used by the mass of the people. But the pottery which has come down to us points to an appreciation of the beautiful, and even to a relatively high standard of well-being among these same country-folk. It is probable that the fabrics and the embroideries of the period were even richer in fine decorative patterns than the pottery itself. Indeed, the small terra-cotta figures of the second and third Bronze periods provide us, in miniature, with fine examples of contemporary clothing and embroidery. The Thracian costumes represented on Greek vases of the classical period should be compared with the costumes of the idols of the Carpatho-Danubian Bronze Age.

The highest forms of luxury and artistic development must, however, be looked for amongst the warrior nobles. Their 'castles' were situated on high ground, not hidden away in inaccessible spots but close to the fertile plains and plateau land, and very frequently on a small hill, or on an island in the middle of a river. These 'castles' were usually defended by ramparts of beaten earth. Sometimes we find walls also, but these are clumsily constructed out of very large irregular

blocks, held together as in the Celtic Iron Age.
The warriors were armed with swords, daggers
and lances, and were protected by breastplates
and shields. They wore helmets and greaves and
fought in two-wheeled war chariots, like those of
the Achaean heroes. Their principal delight, however, was to adorn their bodies with bracelets,
necklaces, rings and pendants, and to decorate
their clothing with all sorts of ornaments. Buttons
and pendants were sewn or fixed on to their clothing, while mantles and tunics were held together
by *fibulae* of extremely varied form and size. Very
typical in this respect are the *fibulae* with many
spirals, or again those in the form of a shield with
large spirals, whose dimensions are frequently
quite extraordinary, some being more than thirty
centimetres long. Their girdles were decorated
with metal plates, generally of geometric design,
engraved or worked in repoussé. The harness and
the bits of their chargers were also adorned with
patterns and metal ornaments. The women wore
bronze or gold earrings of varied forms, bracelets
and necklaces, *papillote* rings, pins for holding
up the hair or clothing, diadems, girdle-buttons,
and other ornamental discs.

The very wealthy, like the Atridae of the Mycenaean world, wore ornaments of pure gold, while
their vases were also of the same precious metal,

as witness the finds at Bihor, Biia and Vŭlchi
Tŭrn (in Bulgaria). The gold itself was of Transylvanian origin and rather pale on account of the
silver which entered into its composition. The less
wealthy nobles—the Odysseus or the Nestor of
their time—had ornaments which, like their
weapons, were made of bronze. Everywhere in
the finds of the Carpatho-Danubian Bronze Age
we come across enormous numbers of sickles.
This would seem to indicate that the nobles of the
Carpathian 'mediaeval period' engaged in agriculture and were not merely owners of large herds
of cattle, or breeders of horses, like the Thracians
of the South. Indeed Déchelette has even advanced
the theory that the sickle was invented by the
Carpatho-Danubians—the people he calls the
Thracians of Hungary.*

In the Carpathians, as in the Celtic West and
the Germanic North, the nobles worshipped celestial beings, among whom we must certainly reckon
the sun god, with his symbols—the disc, the wheel,
the bark, and the swan—this Hyperborean Apollo
to whom the Hellenic legends refer when speaking
of the cult of the sun and the swan amongst the
northern peoples. On the other hand, if we may
judge by the small figures in ware or in bronze
representing men or animals, and above all by

* Déchelette, *Manuel*, i, p. 17 sqq.

the female idols, all of which have been found in Bronze Age sites, we cannot but conclude that the mass of the people had very strong sympathies for the chthonian cults. This religious dualism does not necessarily imply a difference in the ethnic origin of the two social classes amongst the Carpatho-Danubians. It is much easier to suppose that the lower classes, as in the Hellenic South, were much more easily influenced by the ancient native religions which were in honour amongst the pre-Indo-European inhabitants in the very earliest phase of the Neolithic period. The Indo-Europeans, who settled down later amongst the native population of the Carpathians, naturally took over many of their beliefs and superstitions.*
As in Greece, the original inhabitants were gradually denationalized, but their principal cult, that of the great chthonian goddess of reproduction, vegetation and death, was preserved no less tenaciously by the newcomers.

When the Italo-Illyrian merchants, some centuries later (about 1000 B.C.), began to bring the fine bronze products of Atestine, Villanovan and Etruscan workmanship to the Carpatho-Danubians, as well as to the peoples of Central and Western Europe, the nobles of Dacia hastened to

* The evidence is quite clear in this respect in Helladic Greece and in Minoan Crete.

purchase from them their *cistae, situlae,* cauldrons
and goblets, and still more their new types of
armour—breastplates, helmets, greaves and so
on, all embellished with characteristic relief ornaments done in repoussé. In their turn, the native
bronze workers at Spălnaca on the river Mureş,
at Fizeşul Gherlii on the river Someş or at Guşteriţa near Sibiu, followed the new Italo-Hallstatt
models and modified the decorative patterns of
their girdles and bronze discs, and, in some places,
of their armoury work as well. The potters of the
Carpathian lands also reproduced, in clay, the
metal vases which came to them from the south-
west. From this we may conclude that the inhabitants of the Carpathians entered upon the first
millennium B.C. in a period of peace and the greatest economic prosperity.

We do not yet know the details of the events
which took place between 900 and 600 B.C. What
stands out most, however, is the almost complete
absence, in the Carpathian regions, of arms and
other Hallstatt products made of iron. The first
iron weapons which appear here are Scythian
daggers and short swords, and this fact is most
significant. When the Cimmerians, forced on by
the Iranians of the Caspian Steppe, began to migrate towards the Caucasus and Armenia on the
one hand, and towards the Carpathians and the

Balkans on the other (1000 to 900 B.C.), Dacia was profoundly disturbed by them, and many gold and bronze treasures were buried to save them falling into the hands of these invaders. The well-being of the natives nevertheless continued without any very great modifications. The proof of this is given us in the discovery of authentic productions of the fourth Bronze period side by side with articles of 'Scythian' workmanship in the same tombs as, for example, at Aiud[9]. A further proof, of a much more general character, provides decisive confirmation. Between 900 and 600 B.C. we are able to observe the formation of a native Carpathian style in the gold ornaments found between the Middle Danube and the Dniester.* Here we see two equally original tendencies, which become apparent at practically the same time; in the first place, the conservative local tendency towards design of a geometric type, derived naturally from the art of the third period of the Bronze Age; and secondly, the beast style tendency, which was an innovation due to Cimmerian or, more generally, to eastern influences. This second tendency was fairly weak and its manifestations still rare down to the year 700 B.C.

* For a detailed study of the evolution of Carpathian objects of adornment see my book *Getica*, p. 324 sqq. and p. 430 sqq. (French résumé, p. 769 sqq.).

The conservative trend, on the other hand, was very tenacious, and determined Carpatho-Danubian forms until the arrival of the Celts.

The catastrophe of the great Bronze Age civilization in the Carpathian regions did not come, then, before 700 B.C. The Scythian iron swords, moreover, show us who, for a time at least, was the victor. The 'mediaeval' knights of the Carpathians were cast down from their war chariots by the dashing horsemen of the Steppe, whose bronze-pointed arrows wounded from afar their European foes, accustomed, as these were, to fighting at close quarters with lance and sword. The victors were Iranians with a strong mixture of Turanian elements, like their descendants of our own days in modern Turkestan. They brought with them the primitive features of nomadic life and the anarchic tendencies of a vagabond horde, and their influence on Dacia was very nearly a tragedy, as we shall show in later chapters.

The victors were called Scythians, Agathyrsi, Sigynnae, and so on. Herodotus assures us, however, that the Agathyrsi of Transylvania were virtually Thracians. To have become so, they must have been there for a very long time, since our analysis has shown us that the civilization of the Carpathian regions had proceeded without a check, from 700 back to at least 1400 B.C. There is

nothing revolutionary in this conclusion, for it has
long been postulated by pre-historic and proto-
historic archaeologists, such as Déchelette, Hubert
Schmidt and Schuchhardt. But the arguments
they advanced were necessarily incomplete and
therefore not very conclusive. An examination of
the entire civilization of the later Bronze period in
the Carpatho-Danubian regions, with reference to
its organic development, had not then been made.
We have here merely pointed out the conclusions,
since we have published elsewhere all the material
upon which these are based. We believe, however,
that it is now no longer possible to doubt that the
people whom we know later as Dacians and Getae
—names which are probably of Iranian origin,
though the peoples themselves were Thracians—
inhabited the Carpathians from as early as the
middle of the second millennium B.C. The Villanovans therefore constitute the first Italic wave
in Dacia, and the fourth period of the Carpatho-
Danubian Bronze Age was the first period of
western influence in these regions.

Chapter II

CARPATHO-DANUBIANS AND SCYTHIANS

ABOUT the year 1000 B.C., as we have seen, the Carpatho-Danubian countries were inhabited by a northern branch of the Thracians. The dominant forms of civilization were still those of the Bronze Age, the fourth period of which, at once the last and most brilliant, was just beginning. Adjoining these Thracians of the Carpathians came the Cimmerians, who inhabited the whole of South Russia from the Dniester to the Kuban territories. The most recent hypothesis is that this people also belonged to the Thracian family, but the question is, as yet, by no means settled. The Bronze Age civilization of the Cimmerians was, in any case, very similar to that of the Thracians of the Carpathian lands. It appears, moreover, that the Cimmerians had already settled to the north of the Black Sea as early as the sixteenth century B.C.

At about the same period (1600 B.C.) the great western migrations of the Aryans and Iranians of Central Asia began. These peoples came first to Mesopotamia, Syria and Asia Minor, where they are mentioned in the cuneiform texts of the fifteenth century B.C.: and then penetrated, north of the Caspian, into the steppes of Southern Russia. Rostovtseff believes that these Scythians of the Russian Steppe were pre-Zoroastrians, while Vasmer has attempted to show that their language was pre-avestic. On the other hand, during the height of the southern invasion of the Cimmerians through the gorges of the Caucasus, we find the names of kings of these peoples which are already Iranian, such as Šandakšatru, Teušpa, and possibly Dygdamis.* We are inclined to think, therefore, that the current theory that the Scythians did not come into contact with the Cimmerians until the eighth century B.C. at the earliest is not borne out by the known facts. What is more astonishing is that a definite date in an ancient chronology has come down to us as marking the beginning of these Cimmerian invasions caused by the pressure which the Iranians had begun to exert in the neighbourhood of the Caspian. This is the year 1076 in the Eusebian chronology, which agrees perfectly with the other indications we have mentioned. Everything thus points to the conclusion that the westward migrations of the Aryans, which began as early as 1600 B.C., led to the establishment of the Iranians also, both to the south-east and to the north of

* We shall also find examples of a Thracian people with kings of Iranian name, in Dacia during the sixth century B.C.

the Black Sea, at a much earlier date than 800 B.C.

It is true that we do not find archaeological evidences for the presence of the Scythians in South Russia which can be dated with any certainty to a period earlier than the seventh century. It is also true that the Iranian migrations into Eastern and Central Europe up to the Oder, the Adriatic and the Aegean, were barely completed by the sixth century. The presence of the Scythians in Central Europe, however, can already be established by the seventh century. It follows, therefore, that Scythian activity must have begun long before this period, for it to be found at one and the same time over so widespread an area. The same tendency, moreover, is true in the case of the Sarmatians at a much later date. These new Iranians were established on the Don long before the fourth century, though they do not appear on the Danube until the second and first centuries. It seems quite probable that the Scythians must also have taken at least 300 years for their migration from the Caspian and the Volga to the Carpathians and the Theiss.

A portion of the treasure belonging to the last Carpatho-Danubian Bronze Age appears to have been hidden during the Scythian invasions. This is confirmed by almost symbolical discoveries like

that of Greco-Scythian mirrors with the ornamental pattern of the 'Siberian' stag, found side
by side with socketed axes of the fourth Bronze
period.

The Scythian nomads, whose advance drove
the Cimmerians and then the Carpathian Thracians still further to the west, brought with them
iron, a very definite civilization of their own, and
art-forms profoundly influenced by elements of
archaic Greek or Asiatic origin. It is precisely
these characteristics, so different from those of
the European Iron Age, which enable us to
identify their lines of advance and to draw up a
map of Scythian sites from the seventh to the
fourth centuries B.C. not merely in Southern
Russia but also in Central and South-eastern
Europe.

Down to the eighth century B.C. the civilization
of the whole Carpatho-Danubian region was that
of the Bronze Age, supplemented, as we have
already shown in our first chapter, by numerous
western infiltrations of the first Italic or Hallstatt
Iron Age. Suddenly, however, this link with the
West was completely broken. There are hardly
any finds of the second Hallstatt period to the
east of the Middle Danube. The Scythians, on the
other hand, do not seem to have had anything
of importance to give in place of the splendid

civilization they destroyed, for there is nothing in the Carpatho-Danubian lands to compare with the magnificence of the Scythian tombs of South Russia. Indeed the Scythian period in the territories we are now considering represents a complete break between the fine native civilization of the Bronze Age and the Getic renaissance of the second Iron Age which, although its basis was local, was nevertheless profoundly influenced by elements of Celtic origin.

Scythian remains are not found equally distributed throughout the length and breadth of the Carpatho-Danubian lands. There are, indeed, vast areas where they are completely absent. The investigations which have been carried out up to the present point to three compact groups of localities in which Iranian finds have been made —Northern Hungary, Southern Transylvania, and the Wallachian plain.

Discoveries in the north-eastern districts of modern Hungary and in Slovakia—at Abauj, Bereg, Szabolcs, Hajdú, Borsód, Nógrád, Heves and Pest (with certain isolated finds in Western Hungary, in the counties of Györ, Komárom and Zala)—point to a very real Scythian domination in the great plain of the Upper Theiss. This lasted for many centuries, from the second Hallstatt phase, in all probability, down to the arrival of the Celts, whose first appearance seems to be noted in the Borsód district towards the end of the fifth century B.C. Tombs and cemeteries, like those at Pilin or Gyöngyös, have yielded authentic Scythian remains. The style of the modest bronze ornaments for chariots and harness, however, is much more closely related to similar objects found in Russia than to those which have been discovered in Transylvania. This is easily explained, since the Scythians of Northern Hungary were never in contact with those of Southern Transylvania, but were themselves, in all probability, a branch of the great stream of Scythian migration which moved through Northern Bessarabia, the Bucovina, Galicia and Silesia, as far afield as Vettersfelde in Lusatian Brandenburg. These Scythians of Northern Hungary must have found their way into the plain of the Theiss over the passes of what is now Slovakia and, above all, over the Jablonitsa pass, which led them down the Theiss into the plain of the Middle Danube. An archaic Greek bronze vase, such as the *hydria* found at Bene[6], must have followed this same route on its journey from the Greek settlements of the Black Sea into Slovakia.

At the same time as this great wave of Iranian migration to the north, there came yet another and still larger wave, directly from the east. The

route followed traversed Bessarabia and Southern
Moldavia, thence across the passes of the Moldavian Carpathians—and more particularly by that
of Oituz—and so down the valleys of the Mureş
and the Olt. This migration spread through the
broad river valleys of Southern Transylvania, but
did not reach the northern parts of the country.
Scythian remains are, indeed, especially abundant
in the districts of Trei Scaune, Odorheiu, Mureş
Turda, both the Târnave, and Alba de Jos. They
are also to be found to some extent in the counties
of Braşov and Sibiu. The very numerous tombs
of this region, however, have not yielded anything
at all comparable to the splendours of South
Russia. Their contents are usually meagre. The
skeleton is found interred either at full length
and face upwards, or else doubled up on its side.
A few vases—goblets, plates and several pots of
biconical form—have been discovered, but they
are of primitive workmanship and of a type which
is fairly common in our districts. Together with
these, iron daggers and lances and bronze arrow
heads were found. If we add a few bronze bracelets or necklaces and an occasional bronze mirror
in the tombs of the women folk, we have virtually
completed the list. Articles such as the large
horned sword of Hallstatt type at Dobolii de Jos,
which is closely related in point of time to that

found at Kišicky in Bohemia, but whose oriental
zoomorphic decoration proves it to have been of
Scythian origin, are extremely rare. The same is
also true of the pole tops at Ghernesig in the
Upper Mureş valley. The Scythians who settled
in the Wallachian plain appear to have used pro-
cessional chariots much more frequently than did
their fellows in Transylvania, for the museum of
Bucarest alone has many more specimens to show
than all the collections on the other side of the
mountains. The bronze mirrors, with the handle
decorated with the pattern of the crouching stag,
which we find over the whole territory from
Siberia to Transylvania, appear to have been of
Olbian origin, for it was here that the Scythians
of the surrounding districts obtained quite cheaply
the most varied types of products turned out
exactly to suit their taste. The commercial relations of the Olbians with the Scythians of Transylvania must have been very considerable and
were, in any case, much more continuous than
those with the other barbarians to the west or the
north. Indeed the only exact information which
Herodotus was able to obtain at Olbia about the
Scythians of Dacia refers to the Agathyrsi of
Transylvania. It was known at Olbia that, in the
fifth century, their customs were the same as
those of the Thracians—that is to say that they

were completely denationalized—and that they inhabited the valley of the Mureş. This has been confirmed most clearly by the excavations. They were known to have been very rich in gold ornaments, a fact which is also borne out by discoveries made in Transylvania. These do not, however, occur in the tombs of wandering Scythian knights, but in the Hallstatt deposits of the natives, amongst whom the denationalized Scythians, by right of conquest, very soon came to be the dominant class.

A third wave of Scythian migration spread over the whole Wallachian plain. This seems to have passed through into the valley of the Save, and even to have reached the Adriatic. The peoples who took part in this southern migration were known by the Iranian name of Sigynnae. This was noted by Herodotus, and his description corresponds fairly accurately, from the geographic point of view, with the results of the discoveries which have since been made on the spot. As, prior to the publication of my book on the Getae, these discoveries were, for the most part, either unpublished or else inadequately interpreted, it may be as well to enumerate them briefly. The museum of Bucarest has a large hemispherical cauldron two feet in diameter, of the old Scythian type, which was found at Scorţaru. This has eight vertical handles fastened to the rim of the vase, together with two horizontal ones like the bronze *hydriae* of Greek type. One can see traces of the original design, with one central support, as is the case with all Scythian cauldrons, though this one has three feet in the Greek style. From Năeni comes a bronze group which originally had three figures [7]. The central one, a woman, is shown astride a lion, while the other two represent men accompanying her on foot.* This group obviously represents Anaïtis with her two divine acolytes, to whom Strabo refers (XI, 512). From some broken tumulus or other at Bucarest itself we have, amongst other things, a bronze comb [7], of fairly crude workmanship, although it must have been made in a Greek city. It is reminiscent of the fine gold comb of the fourth century B.C. which was found at Solokha on the Dnieper. A tumulus broken open by peasants at Bălănoaia, near Giurgiu, contained an Ionian *lebes* of the fifth century B.C., of Greek workmanship but in use amongst the barbarians. The store of small gold rings, cut in various sizes according to a weight system which Sutzu has attributed to the standard of Cyzicus, found at Turnu Măgurele, also contains some armlets and fragments of gold tubing.

* The right-hand figure has disappeared, but the fragments which have been preserved enable us to see what it was like.

These are Scythian in style and use and probably
belonged to canopy pillars or to sceptres. Somewhere in the neighbourhood of Craiova a fine
silver treasure was found in 1917 during the
German occupation of Roumania. This comprised
various appliques, most of which seem to have
been used as harness ornaments. The treasure
itself was taken by the Germans and is now in
Berlin. Schuchhardt has only published two
specimens in his *Alteuropa* (p. 332)[7]. These
Craiova finds are absolutely identical with those of
Krasnokutsk on the Dnieper, which were published
by Minns (*Scythians and Greeks*, p. 167 sqq. and
p. 267). From Poroina we have a *rhyton* in silver
gilt of the same Greco-Iranian type of workmanship as the Panticapaeum *rhyton* published in the
Antiquités du Bosphore Cimmérien and in Konda-
kov's *Antiquités de la Russie Méridionale*. We
might also enumerate other Scythian objects in
the Bucarest museum, which, although their exact
provenance is unknown, certainly come from the
Wallachian plain[8]. For example, there are four
bronze pole-tops with stag figures crouching on
cones pierced by two rows of triangular holes
(cf. supra, p. 22 n.). These served as ornaments for
the top of canopy supports. Again there is a
bronze standard head in the form of a seahorse
which is a very common design in Greco-Scythian

art; a bronze sheet repoussé in the Greek manner, which may have covered the side projection of a wooden Scythian *gorytos*; the small bronze figure of a crouching ram, for which the most complete analogy may be found in the ram figures which adorn both ends of a gold bracelet in the Oxus treasure (probably of the fourth century B.C.); a piece of harness in bronze representing a hare's head which, incidentally, is quite a common pattern in Scytho-Ionian art, a slide of identical form having been found in Southern Russia; and, finally, a number of other small figures and appliques which we must pass over for want of space. Iranian penetration in the whole Wallachian plain is, in any case, amply established by the examples we have already cited:

Running parallel, as it were, with this third Scythian wave which submerged Wallachia, a fourth wave swept over the Dobruja, Bulgaria and the whole of Thrace up to the Rhodope mountains. The Scythian tombs, which have recently been excavated in Central and Southern Bulgaria, have disclosed a large number of Greco-Scythian objects in gold, silver and bronze. They betray the influence of the genuine models of the Black Sea or Transcaspian regions and their character furnishes us with decisive proof of their origin. It is, of course, an established fact that examples of pure Greek art, whether archaic, classical or Hellenistic, and whether made of gold, silver or bronze, are found everywhere, and Scythia is no exception to the rule, since these were the natural complement of native or mixed handiwork.

The tombs of Brezovo and Panagyurishte, near Philippopolis, and those at Bedniacovo and Radyuvene appear to have contained truly royal contents similar to those of Southern Russia. We do not know whether their owners were Scythians or Thracians. It is indeed quite possible that they belonged to Thraco-Scythian princes of the fourth century B.C. At that period the pressure of Iranian nomads (Sarmatians) became so strong along the river Don that the Scythian tribes of the valleys of the Dnieper and the Bug started to migrate once again towards the south-east (as witness the case of Ateas). This would naturally lead to a fresh development of Scythian influence in the Thracian world.

Let us compare, for a moment, these four Scythian regions of Central and South-eastern Europe—Hungary and Slovakia, Transylvania, Wallachia and Bulgaria. We are struck at the outset by the very significant fact that the intensity of Scythian influence increases as we approach the warm seas. In the Northern

Carpathians it is merely local and transitory, and
even in Southern Transylvania, although well represented so far as the number of objects found
is concerned, it never succeeded in dominating
the second period of the first local Iron Age. In
Wallachia, however, its affinities with the civilization of the Russian Steppe is sufficiently clearly
marked, while, finally, in Bulgaria there is no
doubt whatsoever as to the identity of Iranian
culture from the Tanaïs to the Hebrus. It would
seem, then, as though the only possible conclusion
would be that these Scythian migrations must
have taken the same general course as the later
movements of Sarmatians, Goths, Bulgars and
the rest, about which we are much more fully
informed. In other words, the general direction
was towards the Balkan Peninsula rather than
towards Central Europe.

These generalities, however, are not sufficient.
We must examine in some detail the Scythian
problem in Transylvania, where contemporary
scholars, almost without exception, regard Iranian
influence as so important that the whole first local
Iron Age is commonly described as the Scythian
Age in Carpatho-Danubian history.

In the last chapter we pointed out that, at the
time of the arrival of the Scythians (circa 700 B.C.),
the Carpatho-Danubian peoples were moving

rapidly towards the Iron Age civilization of the West. Moreover, the whole of the fourth period of the Carpathian Bronze Age had already been profoundly influenced by the forms of the first Iron Age as it developed in Italy and the Alpine lands. The Scythians, arriving with their own type of Iron Age civilization, put a stop to these relations with the West. Let us, therefore, examine what they have left behind them in Transylvania, beginning, as did Herodotus, with the valley of the Mureş, the home of the Aga-thyrsi.

At Târgul Mureşului, which was situated in the midst of a thickly populated district, the finds point to a very rich native civilization of the fourth Bronze Age. Italic influences are observable in the bronze vases and terra-cotta imitations of the Benacci II—Arnoaldi types. There is a Scythian necropolis where the rite of inhumation stands out in marked contrast to that of cremation, which was practised in Dacia from the Bronze Age, and, indeed, in some parts from Chalcolithic times down to the Roman period and even as late as the introduction of Christianity in the fourth or fifth century A.D. The inventory of the tombs is very meagre. There are, in the first place, three types of vase—a biconical urn, in the Villanovan style: a cup, with a single handle

4

raised above the brim: and a very large goblet of
an old local type which goes back to Neolithic
days. There are a few knives of no particular
interest: some bracelets made of thin bronze wire,
with no ornaments, but with conical knobs at
both ends: and some *fibulae* in the form of a bow,
of the common Hallstatt type which is found to
the north no less than to the south of the Danube.
There are no Scythian swords and but a few
bronze arrow heads. Apart from the fact of inhumation, as opposed to cremation, there is
virtually no sign of Scythian influence. The same
can also be said of the tomb at Pişchi.

In the district of Aiud, which was thickly
populated both in the Bronze Age and in the
Scythian period, there can, however, be no doubt
as to the Scythian character of some of the tombs.
Four of these have been excavated and are well
stocked with Hallstatt and Scythian specimens[9].
The bronze crosses and rosette crosses are of
western type: the axes, swords and arrow heads
are Iranian—and that is all. The same is true of
Mirislău and Gâmbaş, both of which are in the
same region. Swords, lances and double-headed
axes are primitive in their workmanship and
barbarian in form, while the pottery is of local
character. We find the rite of inhumation at
Gâmbaş in both its forms; some bodies being laid

out straight while others are doubled up. At Murgeşti, to the south-east of Târgul Mureşului, the Scythian warrior who was found intact in his tomb, had taken with him to the other world a lance, a sword and thirty arrows—and nothing else. Still further to the south, at Jacul Român, the tomb of a woman was found to contain a mirror with the typical Scythian *motif* of a crouching stag and a wolf. Another mirror, of very rustic workmanship, and probably of local origin, has been found at Proştea-Mică. It is ornamented with the Hallstatt geometric pattern of an encircled cross. The 'Scythian' tombs at Rodbav, Jidveiu and Blaj add nothing to what we have already said. Mirrors have also been found at Păuca, Ghindari and Feiurd, while arrow heads have been discovered in many places. It would, however, be somewhat naïve to attribute all the arrows to Scythian warriors and all the mirrors to Scythian women. These mirrors, which repeat, with monotonous regularity, the type which we have already described, were imported from the Greek cities of the Black Sea, and, above all, from Olbia. They offer no evidence whatsoever as to Iranian workmanship in Dacia, and, when found side by side with a buried body, they do not even afford any proof as to the nationality of their owner.

In the whole Carpathian region north of the
Transylvanian Alps there are only two places
where Scythian cones, as ornaments to the tops
of canopy supports for ceremonial chariots, have
as yet been discovered. These are at Ghernesig,
in the upper valley of the Mureş and at Somhid,
in the lower valley of the same river. The pole-top
found at Somhid, however, is of the Gyöngyös
type, and thus belongs to the Scythian group of
the Upper Theiss and not to that of the Mureş.
On the other hand, the engraved lines, the curved
shape and the pattern of the solar bark on the fine
gold necklace found at Rakamaz on the Upper
Theiss show that it has nothing to do with
Scythian art.

If we look at a map of Scythian finds in Dacia
—and we have only quoted the most characteristic of these—we see at once that the Scythians
were far from occupying the whole country. They
represent small enclaves in the midst of the native
population. There was no solid Iranian block in
the territory of the Northern Thracians as there
was, for example, in Southern Russia.

On the other hand, the remains of the Scythian
civilization of the Carpathians are primitive in
character, reducible to a few main types, and
found, moreover, within a very limited circle.
We have short iron swords, which are more like

daggers, sometimes double-edged, sometimes with only one edge in the form of a large, slightly bent knife. The large sword at Dobolii de Jos is quite unique and does not count at all in a general summary. There are also iron lances and double axes of rustic workmanship and primitive form. The arrow heads, however, are not always of Scythian type, for in the Bronze Age deposits we also find some of very closely related form. The barbed, socketed arrow heads, triangular in section,* are probably pure Scythian, though this is not the only type that has been found. With the exception of a rather doubtful fragment from Bucarest, no single *gorytos* has come to light; nor are there any examples of costumes or harness with fine appliques like those found in Russia, with the one solitary exception of that from Craiova. There are two examples of cauldrons, but they both come from a region which we would naturally expect to be Scythian—the one being found at Scorțaru near Braila and the other at Sapohovo in Eastern Galicia. There is an almost total absence of examples of Greco-Scythian art and only two cases of imported Ionian work—the *hydria* at Bene and the *lebes* at Bălănoia. No pottery of typical Scythian form has been found. Simplicity and poverty are indeed the characteristics

* Cf. Minns, *Scythians and Greeks*, fig. 82.

of an Iranian people who lived as it were in
little islands in the midst of a compact Thracian
population. The region of the Mureş is, of course,
an exception to this generalization. Herodotus
refers to the Agathyrsi and we also find oriental
intruders in larger numbers in the tombs of this
region.

Géza Nagy,* however, whose theories as to the
Turano-Mongolian origin of the Scythians have
found some support in Minns' book, has characterized the copper double axe as Scythian, and
the type of axe like the gold axe of Ţufalău as
Agathyrsian. Other scholars, such as Márton and
Hampel, have also regarded the golden treasures
of Gyoma and Firighiaz in the plain of the Lower
Mureş as being Scythian or Agathyrsian. These
opinions need some further consideration.

Nagy admits that these two types of axe are
much older than 700 B.C., the date of the arrival
of the Scythians proper in the Carpathians. He
describes as Scythians, however, a nomad people,
consisting mainly of Finno-Ugrians and Turko-
Tartars, who, according to his view, came to
Europe as early as 1500 B.C. It was they who
spread the primitive pattern and workmanship

* The principal works in which he advances these theories
are *A szkythák nemzetisége* (1895) and *A szkythák* (1909). On
this question see Pârvan, *Getica*, p. 363 sqq.

of copper axes throughout the whole region from the Urals and the Caucasus to Hungary and Troy for upwards of a thousand years. The axes, however, of the seventh city of Troy (of the Trero-Cimmerian period) are made of bronze, while those of Ţufalău are of gold. The types found in the fourth Hungaro-Roumanian Bronze Age are much more complicated and numerous than this theory would lead one to expect. Nagy himself was thus led at one time to consider the possibility of the Cimmerians being responsible for the types to which we refer. We might also point to the Northern Thracians, who inhabited the Carpathians from at least the second millennium B.C., but this would merely be one hypothesis the more. The 'Scythian' theory as to the origin of these 'Hungaro-Roumanian' axes cannot be established.

Let us turn, for a moment, to the treasures found at Gyoma and at Firighiaz. In the first-named locality a mortuary chamber constructed of large beams, as in Southern Russia, was discovered in a tumulus, and this fact seemed to point to a Scythian tomb. The tomb itself, which collapsed during the excavations, was found to contain a certain number of gold objects. These were published later by Márton[11], together with a detailed commentary in which he endeavoured to establish their Scythian character. In view of the exceptional nature of this tomb, so rich in gold when compared with the Scythian tombs of Dacia and the Northern Carpathians, which are generally 'modest and poor', Márton feels obliged to look for analogies in the Scythian tombs of Southern Russia. Such a comparison, however, is not very helpful owing to the fact that Greek art had profoundly modified both the local geometric designs and the naturalism of these Asiatic peoples. Indeed the analogies established amongst the Scythians of Southern Russia merely confirm the impression of a barbarian, Hallstatt style which strikes one immediately one sees the treasure of Gyoma. Its only decorative line is the zigzag, and this is an old Central European pattern. The small gold buttons for sewing on to garments are identical with those we know to belong to the last period of the Carpatho-Danubian Bronze Age. Indeed, as Márton himself has shown, the ring of many spirals is reminiscent of the finds at Pereceiu. A few other objects, together with the funeral rite itself, would seem to point to the Scythians, though even so the oriental elements in the Gyoma treasure are very slight.

It is strange that the rich treasure from Firighiaz, on the left bank of the Lower Mureş, which contained a large number of gold bracelets, should ever have been attributed, even by way of hypothesis, to the Agathyrsi. Márton, who published the finds, has very properly insisted on the local character of the forms. These comprise bars of quadrangular shape thinned out at both ends: bars of the same general shape, but terminating in inverse spirals at both ends: and, finally, bars of semi-cylindric form with developments into double scroll spirals at both ends. All three are typical of the Carpatho-Danubian Bronze Age. The dotted lines which ornament these bracelets and the excessive use of the spiral both point to the Hallstatt period. Márton ascribes this treasure to about the ninth century B.C. and this date is confirmed by a whole series of stylistic considerations which we have formulated in connection with the evolution of the Firighiaz forms in the country occupied by the Northern Thracians. Indeed, work in gold, which flourished in Dacia more especially during the fourth period of the Transylvanian Bronze Age, reached its highest point of artistic development before the Scythian invasion. The difference in style, however, between the bracelets of Firighiaz on the one hand, and that found at Bellye on the other, together with the intermediary forms found at Fokorú, Szoboszló, Săcheihid, Pipea [10], Biia and Dálj, forces us to assume that the evolution from the one type to the other must have been spread over a considerable period of time. If therefore we may ascribe the Bellye treasure to the end of the sixth century at the latest, we may well conclude that that of Firighiaz belongs at least to the ninth century.

The style of the gold ornaments of the fourth period of the Carpatho-Danubian Bronze Age is so striking that the bracelets with spiral-shaped ends found in Bohemia and even in Prussia have rightly been attributed to one and the same source of inspiration—the industrial art of the Carpathians. If, in addition to these ornaments, we consider also the gold vases, which, unlike the bronze ones, were not imported from Italy but were actually made in Dacia, we shall no longer be in the least surprised at the secondary rôle played by the Scythians in this region. In point of fact, the Dacian jewellers were following an ancient tradition derived from the native 'bronze' style. To this they added patterns of Italic, as well as of Central European, origin. All, however, had the unity of Italo-Danubian civilization in the Bronze Age as their point of departure. In this connection we might cite the pattern of large bosses surrounded by concentric circles done in repoussé which developed along parallel lines in the case of a bronze Atestine cauldron found near Stettin, and in that of a Dacian gold goblet found at Biia; or that of handles finishing in double scroll spirals, like the bracelet ends of the period, in true local style, or yet again the lines dotted in an ancient style, both primitive and naïve, which we find on bronze girdles from Spălnaca, Suseni and elsewhere. The fluted pattern was quite as widespread, even in the first Iron Age. It was known to the Carpatho-Danubians as early as the Chalcolithic period, as the goblets found at Ariuşd and at Bonţeşti clearly show. Ornamental flutings, whether vertical, oblique or horizontal, were very fashionable in the Bronze Age and are also found in Transylvania, no less than in Dalmatia, during the first Iron Age. It is true that the gold vases from the Bihor district with their decorative flutings, belong to a slightly older period than the vases and bracelets at Biia, with their concentric circles and lines of bosses[10]. The two patterns, however, may be found together at an even later date.

The fact is that, during the first Iron Age, Dacia was influenced by many and varied tendencies. Take, for instance, the so-called 'Scythian' treasure at Ţufalău, with its 'Cimmerian' gold axes and its appliques with spiral ornaments of almost Mycenaean character: the gold convex

discs found at Şmig, with the ancient Chalcolithic
decorative pattern of the four-branched helix:
the vases and bracelets found at Biia, which we
have just described: or, again, the zoomorphic
'Cimmerian' treasure of Mikhalkovo, to which we
shall return later. Even these few examples
suffice to show that it is first and foremost the old
and rich native civilization of the Bronze Age:
then, but to a much smaller degree the Villanovan
elements: and, finally and quite by way of
exception, the Asiatic Caucasian patterns, which
determined the forms of Carpatho-Danubian
civilization in the first Iron Age.

Of course there were a whole series of cultural
and artistic influences—first of 'Cimmerian' and
later of Iranian origin—which give quite a special
character to the Carpatho-Danubian Iron Age
when viewed as a whole. We are only concerned,
for the moment, with oriental features in Dacia
during the Hallstatt period, reserving the Scythian elements of the La Tène period for consideration in Chapter IV.

It is not a mere accident that the treasure of
Mikhalkovo in Galicia should find its counterpart
at Dálj in Slavonia, or even at Pashaköi in Bulgaria
on the one hand, and at Fokorú in Northern
Hungary on the other. These are all in the Hallstatt sphere of gold work. Nor is it surprising

that similar finds should have been made in yet
another absolutely contrary direction at Ananyino
in North-east Russia, or even in the Caucasus.
The fact is that, about the year 1000 B.C., the
Geto-Cimmerians formed a world of their own,
with regular relations in the economic and cultural
sphere, from the Alps to the Caucasus. Cultural
forms which originated in Western Asia could
easily find their way into the heart of the Getic
lands of the Northern Carpathians or the Danube
valley. This accounts for the *fibulae*[11] with zoomorphic plates in the Caucasian style which have
been found both at Mikhalkovo and at Dálj, as
well as the vase from Pashaköi. On the other hand,
Hallstatt forms and workmanship in the treat-
ment of metals penetrated far into Poland and
Russia. This, of course, is responsible for the close
stylistic resemblances between the treasure of
Fokorú and that of Mikhalkovo. The zoomorphic
style of all three—Mikhalkovo, Dálj and Pashaköi
—is much closer to the Caucasian forms of the first
Iron Age, or indeed to such Getic forms as the
standard with a wolf's head, wide-open jaws and
a long dragon tail (see infra, p. 124 sqq.), than it is
to Greco-Scythian elements, whether in the developed Ionian style, or in the naïve forms of the
Iranian nomads, with their obvious sympathy for
animal life.

We must bear in mind, therefore, this first eastern aspect of Carpatho-Danubian civilization which came long before the advent of the Iranians and which even continued to make its influence felt after the arrival of the Scythians. The treasure at Mikhalkovo may well belong to the Scythian period, but it is not Scythian in style. The origin of these Cimmero-Asiatic influences should probably be dated back to a period even earlier than the year 1000 B.C., as we shall show later by other evidence.

The Scythians, who were a people of wandering bowmen, lived by raising cattle and horses, the latter being the more important, and did not develop any very advanced forms of civilization. The Getae of Dacia, on the other hand, whose cultural life was superior to theirs both in quality and in antiquity, were, above all, agriculturists. In order to defend themselves against the Scythians, they also became mounted bowmen, at any rate in the Moldavo-Wallachian Steppe, and it is in this character that we read of them in Thucydides as early as the fifth century B.C. From the Scythians also they learned the tactical formation of battle-order in the shape of a wedge, with the object of breaking through the enemy front. These Geto-Scythian knights, like the Geto-Celts of a late period, thus acquired common tastes, pre-occupations and habits which also made themselves felt in certain manifestations of Geto-Scythian art.

The naturalism of the nomads of the Steppe did much to modify the geometric patterns of the agriculturists of Dacia. The Scythian tombs of Northern Hungary, like those of Transylvania, have been found to contain spiral-shaped rings, with smooth or indented stems, one of the two free ends being in the form of a fantastic animal such as the dragon or the serpent. These apotropaic creatures, themselves Turano-Siberian varieties of old Mesopotamian monsters, are also found at Pilin in Hungary, no less than at Minussinsk, Ananyino, on the Oxus and at Susa. They provided the model for Dacian gold bracelets like that found at Toteşti and, in consequence, initiated a new decorative tendency in Daco-Getic silver work during the La Tène period.

Similarly, the zoomorphism of the Ionians, which was adopted in its entirety by the Scythians of Southern Russia, was also destined to spread throughout Dacia, either in its purely Greek form, or else in Iranian imitations. At Muhipuszta in the Upper Theiss valley, for example, a native terra-cotta vase with a zoomorphic handle has been found. The original of this must have been a Greek bronze vase which came to Northern

Hungary by the same route as the fine Ionian *hydria* of the sixth century B.C. found at Bene. There was a regular Scythian trade route connecting the Greek cities of Russia with what is now Czechoslovakia. This led through the Ukraine, Northern Moldavia, Galicia and over the passes of the Northern Carpathians. The originals of the provincial Carpatho-Danubian *fibulae* of the later Roman Empire—in the form of a *svastica* with four heads of horses chasing after each other—are to be sought in the decorative art of the Scythians. As an example we might cite the silver appliques used as ornaments for the harness or bridle bits of the horses of Scythian chieftains at Krasnokutsk on the Dnieper and at Craiova on the Jiu. These Roman provincial *fibulae*, of which typical examples have been discovered in Roman camps at Cristeşti on the Mureş and at Bregetio in Pannonia have nothing in common with the new Sarmatian style such as we find it, for example, at Pásztó in Northern Hungary. The way in which the same subject was treated in the fourth century B.C. and in the fourth century A.D. is completely different. The Roman *fibulae* are of Scythian and not of Sarmatian origin. In this connection 'Scythian style' really refers to those Greco-Asiatic forms which flourished in Eastern

Europe between the eighth and the sixth centuries B.C. From this point of view it should be remembered that the Carpatho-Danubian peoples had been subjected to this influence under the Cimmerians, considerably prior to the advent of the Scythians.

Problems of Dacian civilization, such as the question of the Dacian standard or the yataghan, cannot be solved by merely considering pure Iranian elements. The whole trend of oriental influence in Dacia from the Cimmerian period at the end of the second millennium B.C. must be borne in mind. Indeed a most interesting chapter in a proto-history of the Carpatho-Danubian lands would be that dealing with copper work in Dacia during the Bronze Age and the first Iron Age and investigating the origin of the types of arms and tools not only in copper but even in gold as well. Such a study would furnish still further examples of the way in which zoomorphic patterns, of Asiatic origin, were transformed into geometric designs in Dacia, though not to the extent of obliterating the original form. Thus the gold axes of Ţufalău (cf. p. 54), or the brass ones found at Batta, betray, in the curious convex wave of the mall broadly spread over the handle, the zoomorphic line of the beast lying in wait which we find on the mall of axe handles in Western Asia.

The general problem of the relationship between Scythians and Carpatho-Danubians, however, can only be approached in a really satisfactory manner by reference to the whole development of civilized life in these parts between the years 1000 and 800 B.C. We must also distinguish clearly between the local and the foreign elements in our general picture of Carpatho-Danubian civilization in the first Iron Age.

During the fourth Bronze period (that is to say the first Hallstatt period), and the Hallstatt period proper (corresponding with the second period in Western Europe), the inhabitants of Dacia were the direct descendants, both in race and occupations, of the peoples of the third period of the Carpatho-Danubian Bronze Age. Wherever fairly complete excavations have been made—as in the districts of Solnoc-Dobâca, Sălagiu, Bihor, Trei Scaune, the Banat, or Buzeu —it appears that Dacia was quite as thickly populated in the fourth as in the third Bronze period. Agriculture was the principal occupation, though work in bronze, gold and copper was also quite common. Silver, on the other hand, only played a very secondary part, and iron none at all. The study of the sites of the fourth Bronze period shows that they were no more than a continuation of those of the third period. It follows that there could have been no serious disturbances in Dacia between 1400 and 700 B.C. The country became increasingly prosperous and the population continued to grow. The arrival of the Scythians, about the year 700 B.C. had the most disastrous consequences. It is true that they did not succeed either in transforming the native civilization or in substituting their own in its place, but actually became denationalized themselves. Nevertheless their constant plunderings combined with the nomadic nature of their life to disturb and to impoverish, during the next few centuries, the flourishing agricultural economy which they had found upon their arrival in these lands.

The Dacian sites of the period between 1000 and 300 B.C. fall into two categories. On the one hand, we find fortresses, situated on commanding heights or in other spots well defended by nature: and on the other hand, the villages. The former have far more to offer in the way of finds, both as to number and quality. They contain many objects in metal and fine pottery, which are typical examples of the latest ruling fashion. The villages, on the other hand, have but little to show. Metal objects are almost non-existent, while the pottery is of so commonplace a type that Neolithic elements are faithfully reproduced even in the second Iron Age. This makes it very difficult to date villages belonging to the fourth Bronze and second Hallstatt period. We are face to face with what is virtually a perpetually primitive age and it is only when we find an occasional fragment of pottery or some quite unexpected form of vase that we are able to get our bearings. What is abundantly clear, however, is that neither the fortresses nor the villages of the Carpatho-Danubian Hallstatt period have anything specifically Scythian to show us.

The large number of bronze swords, daggers and lances found in the deposits of the last Bronze Age in Danubian Europe would seem to point to the existence of a very numerous class of freemen who fought on their own account. They were, in any case, foot soldiers, for only the nobles or the princes possessed war chariots and a complete defensive equipment. It seems probable that, in the great clash with the East, the nobles perished while the masses submitted and engaged in a form of passive resistance which led to a virtual disregard of the intruder. In spite of this warlike aspect of events after the year 1000 B.C., commerce appears to have flourished. Free movement continued from the Black Sea and the Adriatic to the North Sea and the Baltic, as the examples we have given in our first chapter suffice to prove. The arrival of the Scythians put an end to these economic currents for a short time only. They were destined soon to start again and actually to be favoured by the Scythians themselves.

The pomp referred to by Herodotus when talking of the Agathyrsi of Transylvania is most strikingly confirmed by the discoveries made at Țufalău—though this pomp is itself really pre-Scythian in character. The various objects found here in any case enable us to reconstruct something of the life of a proud and wealthy lord of those days. He was clothed in loose-fitting mantles covered with gold appliques—in the form of large convex discs sewn on to the cloth. He appears to have been so proud of the gold he possessed that he armed his halberdiers with battle axes of solid gold when they lined up on ceremonial occasions. The rich lords of Mycenae and of Sparta thus found worthy successors at Țufalău, Biia, Mikhalkovo and Fokorú.

The Cimmero-Scythians were the Dorians of the Carpathians. They plundered the wealth which had been collected together by others, but brought none themselves. Like the Dorians in the South, however, these Scythians of Dacia were not wholly without influence in the development of local civilization. There seem, for instance,

to be reasons for attributing the revival of the
Uranian and solar beliefs which had been so dear
to the Carpatho-Danubians in the Bronze Age
to the advent of this Iranian element in Dacia.
While the Thraco-Phrygians and even the
Greeks themselves adopted more and more the
chthonian cults of the Mediterranean region, the
Getae remained true to the Uranian belief in the
immortality of the soul. Neither the Greeks of
Cyzicus and of Olbia nor Herodotus understood
their religion. The former attributed Pythagorean
legends to the Getae while the latter described
their beliefs with an air of astonishment which he
did but little to conceal. At the time of the
arrival of the Scythians the Carpathian Thracians,
like all northern peoples, worshipped Zalmoxis,
the god of the hidden sky. The sun, the moon, the
shepherd's star, and the heavenly knights accompanying the golden master of the sky on their
war horses, appear to have played at most a very
secondary part. The symbolic representations of
the sun god—the wheel, the swan or the bark—
which the northern peoples acquired from the
Mediterranean world at the beginning of the
Bronze Age, played the same part in the Carpathians as they did everywhere else. As *ex-votos*
or as amulets they recalled to mind the apotropaic
or healing qualities of the sun god. Like the

Celtic Apollo, this Getic Zalmoxis was a 'healer'
God. The Scythians, however, brought with them
a naturalistic interpretation of anthropomorphic
and zoomorphic signs and symbols which they had
learnt first in Asia and then again in Southern
Russia. This is not the place to explain the origin
of the horseman deity of the Thraco-Iranians, of
whom pictorial representations are so numerous
throughout the Danubian lands in Roman times.
It will suffice to point out that the Iranians must
have prepared the way for these religious *motifs*.
Mithras and Anaïtis were known in Dacia before
the advent of the Romans. Diana Regina, the
great Thracian goddess, whom Herodotus refers
to as Ἄρτεμις Βασιληίη in his account of the
Rhodope region, was also worshipped by those
Scythians who lived to the north of the Black Sea.
Thanks to the collaboration of the Greeks, this
deity acquired her definite pictorial representation amongst the Greco-Iranians. It is of course
difficult to advance hypotheses on a subject still
so little known as the comparative religion of
Eastern Europe. The monastic order of ascetics,
called *ktistai* by the Getae (Strabo, vii, 296) and
polistai amongst the Dacians, appears, however,
to have so definitely Iranian and Asiatic a flavour
that it cannot be passed over in silence in this
connection.

Of course, examples of the reverse process are also to hand. In the so-called 'Scythian' burial places at Aiud and at Pişchi on the Mureş, for instance, the corpse is found with a bronze solar wheel on its forehead. This marks the beginning of Getic influence. At a later date, when these peoples had become thorough Thracians, they even burned their dead. Similarly, the Getae themselves, during their sacred games, had come to honour Zalmoxis by fighting by his side against those monsters, disguised as dragons, who covered his luminous face during a storm, not, as of old, with their native lances but with bows and arrows of Iranian origin. These celestial dragons, moreover, were destined to be adopted as the classic *apotropaia* of the Daco-Getic people, and to serve as their war standard.*

Although the migrations of the Scythians put an end, for a century and a half (circa 700–550 B.C.), to relations with the West, there was no break of continuity in the Carpathian lands themselves, between the first and second Hallstatt periods. This is particularly true in the case of the rural life of the country. The nobles, of course, suffered heavily. They were, for the most part, either killed in battle, reduced to serfdom

* Compare what we have to say about this religious symbol in Chapter IV, pp. 124–6.

or else to the status of free commoners. This is
why the second Hallstatt period has no examples
to show of luxury articles imported from the
Illyro-Italic lands of the south-east, as in earlier
days. There are, however, a few archaic Greek
products, though these are very rare and in any
case probably came by way of the Scythians from
the Black Sea and the Aegean. Nevertheless the
North Thracian nobility did not disappear completely. It was merely being reorganized, for in
the La Tène period we shall see it once again in
all its ancient power and glory. This will be the
period of Dacian silver treasures, of great
fortresses built on inaccessible mountain tops,
and of victorious wars against Scythians and
Celts alike. This topic will be considered in a later
chapter. For the moment we must bear in mind
that the first Carpatho-Danubian Iron Age can
only be described as Scythian in the way in which
the last Bronze period was Italic and the second
Iron Age Celtic.

Chapter III

CARPATHO-DANUBIANS AND GREEKS

IT seems increasingly probable that the migrations of the peoples of Central, Eastern and Southern Europe towards the end of the Bronze Age not only put an end to the peaceful development of Mycenaean civilization in Greece, but also interrupted those relations between the Carpatho-Danubian countries and the Hellenic world which had been so important in the earlier Bronze Age. Transylvanian forms of metal work appear in the lands of the Aegean as early as the beginning of the Bronze Age. Moreover, what would seem to be 'Mycenaean' or even 'Minoan' forms are being found in increasing numbers in Carpatho-Danubian work of the second millennium B.C., though research has not advanced sufficiently as yet to enable us to speak with any certainty as to this aspect of pre- and proto-historic times. We must, therefore, confine ourselves to the relations which existed between the Carpatho-Danubians and the Greeks in historic times.

The Greek colonies of the western and northern coasts of the Black Sea are all later than the year 650 B.C. Excavations made at Apollonia in

Bulgaria, at Istria in Roumania, and at Olbia in Russia have yielded nothing belonging to an earlier period than the second half of the seventh century B.C. This was, approximately, the date at which the last invasion into Lydia marked the end of the great Cimmero-Scythian upheaval. Vast Iranian empires were being formed and consolidated in the lands between the Middle Danube and the Don. The native Thraco-Getae, an agricultural people which had settled down long since, accepted the rule of these lords of the Steppe, though they were ultimately to succeed in denationalizing them. In the second half of the sixth century, the high plateau of Transylvania, with the adjoining regions which were in political and economic dependence on it, were under the domination of the Iranian dynasty of Spargapeithes. Agathyrsian in origin, this ruling house had already become Thracianized. In Eastern Dacia, there ruled a certain Ariapeithes, whose centre of influence lay in the country near Olbia. At this latter place, Herodotus acquired a considerable amount of information as to the personal history, the rivalries and the frontier wars of these two kings.

The Dacian lands were very rich and, on the whole, fairly peaceful in the sixth century. As soon as they arrived, the Greeks were able to penetrate in all directions, though we have no information as to their movements in the seventh century. This is not, however, surprising for, even in the Greek cities themselves, finds of the seventh century are few and far between. At that time the activity of these Pontic colonies was only just beginning. The next century, on the other hand, has much of the very greatest importance to show us. From the Kiev region— witness Greek vase fragments of the sixth century found in Podolia—right down to Northern Dacia —where, as we have seen (supra, p. 40), a bronze Ionian *hydria* of the same period was discovered as far afield as Bene in the Slovak Carpathians— the whole of these Geto-Scythian lands were supplied with their manufactured products by the Greeks.

The Danube formed the principal line of advance towards Central Europe. An Olbian *aes grave* bearing the inscription APIX, has been found near the ancient town of Salsovia (the modern Mahmudia) on the banks of the southern arm of the Danube delta. We thus see that this medium of exchange, put into circulation by the Olbians in the sixth century, and of which many examples have been discovered in Russia and Roumania, had also found its way to the Getic bank of the river. Much further up, at Bărboşi, where the Sereth (Tiarantos, Hierasus) joins the main stream, we find a Greek factory situated opposite the old Getic fortress of Dinogetia. Tombs containing black-figure Attic vases establish the period to which this belongs. Finally, an Ionian bronze *lebes* of the fifth century at the very latest, from Bălănoaia in Western Wallachia (supra, p. 44), together with a barbarian treasure of ring money on the Cyzicene standard, of the same period, bear witness to the penetration of Greek ideas and products almost contemporaneously with Iranian forms and certainly much earlier than those of the Celts.

This Hellenic penetration must have been most intensive for the industrial products of the Greek cities to have become familiar even to the primitive native potters. At Muhipuszta on the Upper Theiss we find terra-cotta imitations of a bronze Ionian vase with a zoomorphic handle as early as this same fifth century B.C. In our first chapter we referred to the terra-cotta imitations of Villanovan bronze vases found at Târgul Mureşului. Here we find the process repeated, but with Greek originals coming from the opposite direction.

The importance of direct Hellenic penetration into the territories in the military occupation of the Scythians is not in any way surprising.

Unlike the Celts, who were later to develop, under Hellenic inspiration, an original civilization of their own and to spread it throughout barbarian Europe, the Scythians had no highly developed native culture. Greeks, therefore, were able to work on their behalf and to evolve what we might call a Greco-Scythian style. The Scythian character of these products lies merely in the general inspiration, and not in the workmanship nor the lines nor even always in their practical utilization. Indeed, the great majority of the Scythian kings and princes who had dealings with the Greeks were almost completely Hellenized, as for example, Scyles, son of Ariapeithes, of whom Herodotus speaks. Their ideas of luxury and of comfort were Greek and not in the least barbarian. Moreover, like the contemporary Odrysian kings and most of the petty Thracian rulers of the Balkans at a later date, these Scythian chieftains even regarded it as very fashionable to become thoroughly Hellenized.

The principal rôle in this process of Hellenization naturally fell to the two Greek cities situated on the north-western coast of the Black Sea: to Istria, near the mouth of the Danube (Istros), whose name it bore, and to Borysthenes-Olbia, at the mouth of the Dnieper (Borysthenes). Both flourished under the virtual protection of the great Scythian rulers of Central and Eastern Europe. Their spheres of influence, however, seem to have been defined in such a way that Olbia dominated the trade routes leading across Moldavia or Transylvania to Galicia and Hungary, while the peculiar sphere of Istria was the purely Getic lands of the Danube and its tributaries.

We have already had occasion, in our last chapter, to refer to the close economic and cultural relations which existed between the Scythians of Hungary and Transylvania and the city of Olbia. The routes leading over the Carpathians were either by way of the Slovak passes (Jablonitsa), or else by those of Southern Moldavia (Oituz). As we have seen, these Thraco-Scythians imported the products of Olbian bronze-workers and, above all, ornaments, appliques, mirrors and steel weapons. Fine bronze vases in the purest Ionian style were, however, also much appreciated. This regular commerce of their merchants with the lords of the 'gold country' naturally accounted for the accurate information of the Olbians on matters relating to the Agathyrsi.

Their knowledge of the Danube valley, on the other hand, was very meagre. This was the preserve of the Istrians. Moreover, in the political questions of those days, the Olbians necessarily adopted the point of view of their

direct overlords, the Scythian kings of Western
Ukraine, who sometimes made of Olbia itself
their 'civilized capital'. Further light is thrown
on this matter in the writings of Herodotus, who
visited the settlements of the Pontic Greeks at
least two generations after the foundation of their
commercial and fishing station at Bărboşi, in the
very midst of the Getic lands. In accordance
with the fashion of those days he only became
acquainted with Hellenic Scythia and quite
neglected Hellenic Thrace. He seems, nevertheless, to have gone from Olbia as far afield as
Tyras, though his information as to the country
lying to the west of that place is most confused.
Strangest of all are his references to Istria, which
he describes as being situated exactly at the
mouth of the Danube. The truth is that this city
lay at a considerable distance from the river, as
Flavius Sabinus, governor of Moesia, stated in
a letter to the Istrians written in the year A.D. 44,
καὶ ἐκ τοσούτου διαστήματος ἀφέστηκεν ἡ πόλις ἀπὸ
τῶν τοῦ ποταμοῦ στομάτων.

Herodotus' geographical inaccuracies are, of
course, well known, and need not detain us here.
He did not know the direction of the Danube
even at its mouth, while his enumeration of its
tributaries is completely muddled: rivers of the
left bank being placed on the right bank, and so

on. Of more interest to us are the names which
he gives them. These are all Scythian, for the
Thracian (Getic) forms appear to have been unknown to him. He says that the river which the
Greeks call Πυρετός—a river, we may add,
which flows in Getic territory—is known to the
Scythians as Πόρατα. He only knew the
Scythian name for the Τιάραντος—which is the
Σέρετος of the Getae—and his description of this
river is totally inaccurate. It is clear that those
Greco-Scythians who gave Herodotus this information at Olbia were not in a position to know
anything of the Getic country, which spread west
of Tyras across the mountains, and southwards,
as far as the Thracian lands of the Balkans. Its
ethnographic limits even extended beyond the
river Danube. All that Herodotus learned at
Olbia was that all these countries were Scythian.
That was, of course, quite correct from the
political, but quite wrong from the ethnographic
point of view. It is clear that he would have
obtained much more accurate information at
Istria, if he had taken the trouble to go there.
These sailors and fishermen had, in his day,
already advanced up the Danube to places further
afield even than Bărboşi.

Hellenic penetration in the Danube basin was
thus almost exclusively an Istrian affair. Tomi

only begins to be of some importance in the third century B.C., after the defeat of the Callatians, the allies of the Istrians, who wished to make it a factory of their own. Callatis itself hardly appears to have been really important till the end of the fourth century. It was, in any case, a predominantly agricultural colony which exploited its domains either directly or with the aid of the natives, and engaged in the grain trade. The remaining colonies—Dionysopolis, Odessus, Mesambria and Apollonia—were too far removed from the Danube basin to profit much by opening it up to trade during this early period. It was not, indeed, until the first century A.D. that Mesambria, for instance, was able to enter into relations with Dacia, and the Dacian king Burebista was then the overlord of all the Pontic cities up to Apollonia. The Milesian colony of Tyras, lost in the steppe country of the Tyragetae, was too interested in the fisheries, agriculture and stock raising of a vast area where it had no rival, to take any interest in fisheries and commerce up the Danube valley.

Like the factory of Berezan (at Olbia), and like Apollonia, Istria was founded on an island. The first settlement belongs to the seventh century B.C., a point on which written tradition has been confirmed by the fragments of Ionian and Corinthian vases of this period which we discovered during excavations undertaken in 1915. In the sixth century Istria became a commercial centre of the first rank. On the eastern side of the Acropolis, on the shore of what was then the sea but is now a lagoon, we have found fragments of Milesian, Samian, Rhodian and Corinthian vases, together with statuettes of the goddess with the dove (the so-called 'Phoenician' Aphrodite) which rival, both in number and quality, the fragments of Attic vases with black figures, of the earliest period, discovered on the south-eastern side of the city. These latter were found for the most part in a well shaped like a square funnel and dug out of the solid rock. This is identical in form and purpose with those excavated by Ernst von Stern in the island of Berezan, and by Degrand at Apollonia, on the island of Saint Kyriakos.

Towards the end of the sixth century, Attic influences became predominant on the Thracian coast, and especially at Istria, where excavations have already been carried sufficiently far to enable one to form a general impression. This tendency was felt in the same virtually exclusive manner as at Olbia, Berezan, Panticapaeum, and elsewhere. So far as the vases are concerned, it remains fairly constant throughout the fifth and fourth centuries. It must be noted, however, that Ionic influences are also well preserved in the language of the inscriptions down to quite a late period. We are not now referring to the two dedications to Apollo *Iêtros*—a black marble pedestal for a bronze statue, and the white marble architrave of a temple—both of which belong to the end of the fifth and beginning of the fourth century B.C. These are the oldest inscriptions which have as yet been found at Istria and their Ionic forms are paralleled on the funeral *stelae* of Apollonia which belong to the same period. We are thinking rather of such Ionic forms as ἱέρεως, genitive ἱέρεω, which were still used in these Milesian colonies as late as the first century B.C.

It seems probable that the Greek factory at Bărboşi, which is already referred to in the sixth century B.C., was an exclusively Istrian foundation. It is most unlikely that anyone else would have advanced so far up the Danube or would have known the country well enough to settle there at that early period. The foundation of Istria itself, on the island nearest the Danube mouths which was suitable for the purpose, was undertaken primarily with a view to exploiting the fisheries of the Delta. The very existence of the Istrians seems to have come to depend more and more on their right to fish in the Danube and, more especially, in the Peuce mouth. Freshwater fish and sturgeon, which is most abundant at the actual mouths of the river, must have been the basis of the trade in salted, smoked and dried fish which Istria carried on with the South. When, as part of the kingdom of Thrace, Scythia Minor became a Roman province, the Istrians asked for confirmation of their ancestral rights and actually obtained from their new rulers the privilege of exploiting the Danube fisheries without payment of any tax whatsoever. The reason for this generosity is explained in the letter of the governor Flavius Sabinus (cf. supra, p. 80) which expressly states that practically all the revenue of the city was derived from dried fish. In the sixth and fifth centuries B.C. the Istrians were naturally much more powerful and enter- prising than in the first century A.D. and it seems probable that they exported many other articles besides fish and corn. They certainly sold manu- factured goods to the barbarians and bought skins, honey and slaves from them in return. The routes followed by Menander's Δάοι and Γέται to Athens seems to have passed through the station of Bărboşi and the market of Istria. It is, in any case, quite certain that the Danube, up to its junction with the Sereth, had become a

Greek river by about the year 500 B.C. The merchants of Istria knew the Geto-Scythian country well. They were constantly moving up and down this part of the river with its various branches, channels, lakes and tributaries.

Of course the prosperity of this little Greek world of the Black Sea coast depended to a very great extent upon the individual caprice of the Scythian rulers of the hinterland. Direct penetration by the Greeks themselves occasionally met with such great difficulties as to make it preferable for them to hand over their merchandise to Μιξέλληνες—Geto-Scythians—who would carry it into the heart of the Carpatho-Danubian countries. The attraction exercised by Greek civilization over the barbarians was, however, so irresistible, that the Geto-Scythian kings and princes were often induced to forget their racial origin. This, in turn, naturally led to a national reaction on the part of the barbarians, and was responsible for tragedies like that of Scyles, son of Ariapeithes (Herodotus, IV, 78 sq.).

It was indeed an epoch-making date in the history of Olbia and of Istria when the great Scythian king Ariapeithes, overlord of the colonists of Borysthenes-Olbia, married a Greek woman from Istria (towards the end of the sixth century). Their son Scyles learned the language and literature of the Greeks, and, what was ultimately to prove fatal to him, also embraced the customs and the religion of his mother's people. Herodotus tells us that when he became king, this ruler, in his sumptuous palace at Olbia, was more like a Greek than a Scythian, who should have been living in a tent surrounded by his shepherds and herdsmen. It is natural that he should have felt sympathy with the Pontic colonists, and that relations between his Greek capital of Olbia and his mother's city of Istria should have become much more intimate. But Ariapeithes had been treacherously killed by Spargapeithes, king of the Agathyrsi, in consequence, no doubt, of some border squabble or political rivalry in the lands lying between the Carpathians and the Tyras. Scyles ruled in his father's stead until his subjects rebelled against his Hellenic practices and brought him to his death. The Istrians, meanwhile, had to pay dear for the glory of being related to the Scythian king, whose rival reigned in the Carpathians. Their commerce with the Getae and the Agathyrsi must have suffered greatly from the long-drawn wars between Spargapeithes and Ariapeithes and their respective followers and successors.

Towards the middle of the fifth century, Istria, in common with her sister colonies of the Black

Sea, made great advances in the development of a creative civilization of her own. This upward movement was not seriously checked until the middle of the third century, when the invasion of the Celts shook to its very foundations the whole organization of the barbarian peoples of the Lower Danube. Abundant evidence of this is afforded by the results of the excavations which we have already made amongst the ruins of the city. In the fifth century, Theoxenos, during the eponymous priesthood of his father Hippolochos, son of Theodotos, consecrated a bronze statue to Apollo *Iêtros*. We have found the pedestal, in black marble. The inscription and the cavities on the upper surface, shaped to fit the size and form of the feet of the statue to be fixed there, are both in a state of perfect preservation. A generation later, Xenocles and Theoxenos, nephews of Theoxenos, dedicated a white marble monument to the same god during the eponymous priesthood of their father, Hippolochos, son of Hegesagoras and nephew of the earlier person bearing the same name. This work must have been executed very well and at considerable cost, if we may judge by the architrave bearing the inscription, which has come down to us. From the same period, too, we have a blue marble pedestal which appears to have supported the bronze statue of a certain

Apollonios. This is an example of quite a common practice amongst the Greeks, as we see in fragments containing decrees of the late fourth and early third centuries. They were in the habit of crowning the benefactors of the commonwealth with crowns of gold, ἐν τοῖς ἀγῶσι, and their memory was perpetuated in bronze statues.

The age of Philip, Alexander the Great and Lysimachus is, however, even better represented. About the year 300, the cult of Helios, so typical of Rhodian influence during the Hellenistic period, was taken up with enthusiasm at Istria. In the ruins of the outer wall of the Roman city we have found the marble head of a statue of this god. It is more than twice the size of a man's and the figure must have stood some twelve feet high. It is of excellent workmanship and is a typical example of the style of Scopas. The god wore a rayed crown of bronze which was probably gilded and fixed in the marble by means of tenons. Numerous white marble fragments—columns, architraves, cornices, and so forth—which were used as building material for the construction of the Roman city of Istria are of such dimensions and style that they may well have belonged either to the temple of the sun or to some similar building of this earlier period. On one of the fragments of honorary decrees of about the year

300, we were more than gratified at finding a reference to a Μουσεῖον at Istria.

Other inscriptions which have recently been discovered show that the principal sanctuary was τὸ ἱερὸν τοῦ Ἀπόλλωνος in the Hellenistic period also. Even in the second century B.C. the gymnasium of Istria was full of bronze statues of the benefactors of the city, while the *agoranomoi* erected marble statues to their patron deity Ἑρμῆς Ἀγοραῖος. A fine Apolline relief not only confirms the interest shown by the Istrians in matters artistic during the fourth to the second centuries B.C., but also bears witness to the remarkable ability of their craftsmen. These Greeks, lost in the Thracian North, were people of considerable taste.

Towards the end of the fifth century, the Istrians had begun to strike coins of their own. They were, indeed, the first to do so on the western coast of the Black Sea. Pick believes that all the silver coins of Istria belong to the fourth century. With the possible exception of the reign of Lysimachus, the autonomy of the city remained assured throughout the whole of this period.

The references to Istria in classical literature during these years are somewhat scanty. Such as they are, however, they tend to confirm the

conclusions suggested by an examination of the
results of the excavations which have been
carried out hitherto. We hear of relations
established between the Istrians and the Scythian
royal house of Olbia in the fifth century, as also
of internal revolutions on constitutional matters
referred to by Aristotle, though they took place
before his time. At one period the 'Istrians'—
and this probably refers to the Μιξέλληνες of
Istria under a 'king' of their own—had to wage
war against the Geto-Scythian king Ateas, who
advanced into what is now the Dobruja and was
ultimately driven out by Philip in 339. We hear,
too, of the war fought against Lysimachus in 313
in order to free the city from Macedonian suzerainty, and, again, of the war waged against
Byzantium about the year 260. All this points
to the political and military importance of Istria,
and thus confirms our view as to the wealth and
power of the city.

It is true that, after the days of Philip, the
Pontic colonies came under the influence of the
Greek kings of Macedonia or of Thrace, and that
this relationship lasted for nearly half a century.
From the point of view of penetration into Getic
territories up the Danube valley, however, the
Istrians gained considerably thereby. The bar-
barians of the hinterland were forced to respect

their merchants as being at the same time representatives of the powerful Macedonian kings.

From the sixth century onwards, however, the Istrians, in common with the Greeks of the northern coast of the Black Sea, intermingled, to some extent, with the natives. The Olbians were Greco-Scythians and, in a similar manner, no doubt, the Istrians must have been Greco-Thracians, or, still more probably, Greco-Getae. In the quadrangular well which lies to the south-east of the acropolis at Istria we have found, side by side with pure Greek vases of the sixth century, fragments of very large native vases.* These are in the form of *pithoi*, made by hand out of a very coarse clay, badly kneaded and badly baked. They are decorated with large horizontal circles in relief, covering the vases like the hoops of a cask, while the lines themselves are broken by small oblique notches in imitation of large hempen ropes. The barbarian remains of the second Iron Age, found in the lower town of Istria (to the west of the Acropolis), mixed up, as they are, with Hellenistic fragments, likewise show that the barbarians and Greeks lived together in the town itself as well as in the adjoining countryside.

* von Stern made a similar discovery at Berezan.

This partial fusion of the two peoples enabled the Greeks to establish a whole series of small settlements along the western shore of the Euxine. Their names have not been preserved to us in any written document, but archaeological remains still bear witness to the intensity of Hellenic life in this region.

These same relations of friendship or, at least, of mutual toleration, between Greeks and barbarians, also enabled the citizens of Istria and Tomi and, to a lesser degree, those of Callatis, to pass westwards through Scythia Minor without let or hindrance. A few hours' journey on horseback, and not much more than a day's march with ox-waggons laden with merchandise, brought the Istrians to Carsium and the Tomites to Axiopolis, which are both situated on the Danube. Although this route is very direct, it cannot, however, have been satisfactory for such merchandise as was to be sold much further afield than Carsium or Axiopolis themselves. The constant loading and unloading would actually have been disastrous to commodities like wine. This explains the marked preference accorded to the sea route, which led from Istria, through lake Halmyris into the Peuce arm and thence up the Danube and its various tributaries—the Pruth, Sereth, Ialomiţa, Argeş, and Olt.

With the expeditions of the Macedonian kings against the Geto-Scythians, Philip coming first in 889, to be followed by Alexander four years later, and the fierce wars waged over the turn of the century by Lysimachus against Dromichaites, the powerful Getic king of the Moldavo-Wallachian plains, the Carpatho-Danubian peoples make their first appearance in Greek history proper. Hellenic penetration became as important in these regions as it had already become in Thrace. The great exporters of Greek wine and oil, coming first from Thasos and Rhodes, and then, later, from Cnidos, spread all over the Danube basin. The native Daco-Getae became accustomed to the use of silver money, and commercial transactions appear to have been concluded between the newcomers and the natives even in the smallest and most remote villages of Dacia. The fragments of Greek *amphorae* are often as common as the native relics of this period (La Tène, II and III).

Coming first to Bărboşi, the old Hellenic factory of the sixth century, the first large valley opening a way for these Greek merchants into the lands of the 'Agathyrsi' was that of the Sereth. The shortest route linking up Scythia Minor and the mouths of the Danube with the gold country of Transylvania ran along this river as far as its

junction with the Trotuş, and then up the Trotuş
and over the Oituz pass. On the sharp escarp-
ment of the left bank of the Sereth, at the point
where it is joined by the Trotuş, there stands the
pre-historic citadel of Poiana. Here we have
discovered traces of a number of Thasian *amphorae*, amongst many Daco-Celtic remains. One
of these is in an excellent state of preservation
and the stamp shows that it belongs, at the very
latest, to the third century B.C. The crumbling
slopes of the river bank at this point have also
been found to contain very numerous fragments
of Greek *amphorae*.

The next Hellenic station up the Danube which
has hitherto been discovered is Carsium. This
Getic citadel commanded the valley of the
Ialomiţa, or Naparis as it was then called. As
at Poiana, the only relics of the Geto-Greek
period which have hitherto been found consist of
amphorae. Some of these are well preserved,
though most of them are only in fragments. The
stamps on the handles, which have fortunately
been unearthed, show that they come from Rhodes
and Cnidos. These marks are very well preserved
and may be ascribed with fair certainty to the
third century B.C. The real importance, however,
of Carsium to the trade route running up the
Naparis valley only becomes apparent when we

examine the pottery found at the Greco-Getic station of Piscul Crăsanilor, more than sixty miles further upstream. As at Istria 200 years earlier, Hellenic industrial products were used at Crăsani in the fourth century by a population whose technical knowledge was in a much more backward state than that of the Greeks. Greek *amphorae* are, as elsewhere, much to the fore. Delian goblets were imitated by the natives, and the original mould was found during excavation. Coins of Macedonia Prima, of the period 158– 150 B.C. have been discovered side by side with Daco-Celtic money. Greek lamps, vase fragments in coloured glass, and in particular, a fine three-branched bronze candelabra, swell the total of Greek products found in the midst of Celto-Getic remains at Crăsani.

Still further up the Danube, on an ancient pre-historic site, the Greeks founded the city of Axiopolis. This was an official settlement, established possibly by Lysimachus himself. The excavations made by the late M. Tocilescu and by the Germans during the Great War have established the continuity of civilized life at this spot from the Hellenistic era right down to Byzantine and Bulgarian times. Axiopolis seems to have been chosen with a very definite strategic purpose. It was to form a barrier against the

Getae of the vast Wallachian plains and to protect Greek commerce up and down the Danube. It also covered the land route from Tomi, and was nearer that city than was Carsium to Istria. Handles of Rhodian *amphorae*, with stamps of the third to the first century B.C., have also been discovered here, and point in the same direction as do the corresponding finds made at Bărboşi, Poiana, Carsium and Crăsani. Indeed the same phenomena reappear constantly. There are many Daco-Getic settlements of the second and third La Tène periods which were founded on much older sites. The typical evidences of Hellenic penetration—*amphorae*, Delian or Attic ware, statuettes, vases in coloured glass, bronze or terra-cotta lamps, and so on—have been unearthed in almost all of them. It will suffice to mention Boian, Mănăstirea, Piscul Coconilor, Spanţov, Căscioarele and Zimnicea, on the Danube itself, and Tinosul on the Prahova, in the heart of the Wallachian plain.

The most essentially Getic river, however, was the Argeş, whose name has remained the same, even as to pronunciation, for over 2000 years. Once the Greek merchants had arrived at its mouth they did not hesitate to work their way up this river and its tributaries right to the very gorges of the Carpathians. Of these tributaries perhaps the most important is the Dâmboviţa (on which the modern city of Bucarest is situated), for it leads up to the pass of Bran, which is on the main trade route between Transylvania and Wallachia. The Dâmboviţa formed a principal artery for commercial relations between the Greeks and the Dacians. Along its course several striking discoveries have already been made. At Bogaţi a treasure of Macedonian and Thasian tetradrachms has been found. In the ruins of the castle of Stoeneşti, which was also an important fortress in the Middle Ages, the inscription ΗΡΩΝΟΣ was discovered on the handle of a (pre-Roman) Greek *amphora*. This is not surprising since at that period gold was being worked very intensively at Gemenea, which is only a few miles away. Indeed quite an appreciable quantity of gold is still found there in the alluvial deposits of the Dâmboviţa. The Dacians appear to have turned this gold into annular money, in the form of small gold rings such as those at Turnu Măgurele and elsewhere. This did not, however, prevent them from using considerable quantities of Macedonian and, later, of Thasian coins. We find these tetradrachms, either as originals or native imitations, almost everywhere in Dacia, though they are naturally most numerous on the banks of the Danube or along the routes leading up to that river. We have discovered treasures of Thasian tetradrachms in the old Geto-Greek station at Zimnicea and again at Tărtăşeşti, which is situated in the valley of the Dâmboviţa, some sixty miles away from the Danube, on the route which leads to the Bran pass. Similarly, several hundred Macedonian coins—*drachmae* and tetradrachms of the kings—have been found in the vineyards near Giurgiu, together with coins of the Greek cities of Thrace. From Comana-Vlaşca we have 300 Getic silver coins in imitation of the staters of Philip II; while at Popeşti (Ilfov), copies of Thasian tetradrachms were discovered, one of them with the interesting inscription: ΗΡΑΚΛΕΟΤΣ ΣΩΤΗΡΟΣ ΘΡΑΚΩΝ.

Numismatic evidence enables us to follow the process of Greek penetration stage by stage. We discovered an Olbian *aes grave* of the sixth century in the delta country. Cyzicenes of electrum next make their appearance at Axiopolis. Silver coins struck at Istria, Apollonia and Mesambria followed the same route and are to be found in many places on the Lower Danube. At a later period they found their way into Transylvania and have been discovered in Dacian strongholds like that of Costeşti. By the fourth century, however, Macedonian gold and silver currency had gained the upper hand completely.

In the third century, the Pontic colonies found themselves supplanted by the commercial republics of the South, with Rhodes at their head. These Thasian coins had now acquired a dominant position. Finally, in the second century, the coins of Macedonia Prima penetrated as far as Northern Transylvania.

Moldavia and Wallachia, together with the Dobruja, are extremely rich in treasures of Macedonian money (Philip II, Alexander). More typical still, however, is the large number of finds of Getic tetradrachms—barbarian imitations of the silver coins of Philip II.

The Thasian tetradrachms, which were the last to arrive, spread the furthest to the north and the west. They served as models for a large number of Dacian imitations in Transylvania, though these latter are singularly poor in metallic content. The spread of these tetradrachms runs parallel with commercial penetration, as evidenced by the *amphorae* which have been discovered in all the sites of the third to the first century B.C., in the Getic territory to the south and east of the Carpathians.

There are no intelligible inscriptions on any of the Dacian coins, although there were on all the originals on which they are based. Most of these originals, indeed, were Macedonian silver coins of

CARPATHO-DANUBIANS AND GREEKS 101

Philip II, or else Thasian tetradrachms. So long as there were sufficient originals, there was no need for imitations. At the time and place, however, in which these imitations were struck, the peoples were so barbarous that they could no longer read the original inscriptions.

The Thasians came as peaceful merchants. Philip, on the other hand, appeared as the lord of the Dacians of Scythia Minor, and as a very embarrassing neighbour along the Danube frontier. In both cases, however, the result was the same: the Dacians were brought into contact with the Greek world. This fact also elucidates another chronological problem. In the earliest period (from the seventh to the fifth centuries) the Istrians were the only Greeks who visited the Getae, though these latter people were as yet too barbarous to be influenced in a lasting manner. In the Hellenistic period (from the third to the first centuries), the Rhodians had taken their place. They penetrated everywhere, playing the same rôle in the Danube basin as did the Venetians in mediaeval times. In point of currency, however, these lands had already become a preserve, as early as the fourth century, for the gold coins of Philip and, later, of Alexander and Lysimachus, and for the silver money first of Macedonia and then of Thasos.

Unfortunately, excavations in the Dacian fortresses of the Carpathians have not yet advanced far enough for us to attempt to describe the cultural relations which must have existed between the Geto-Agathyrsi and the Pontic Greeks in the sixth and fifth centuries B.C. The structural style of the Getic mountain fortresses, to which we shall refer in our next chapter, embodies many archaic elements, which point to the closest of relations with the South. Can it be that Spargapeithes had summoned Greek master-builders to his aid? or are these similarities nothing more than survivals of the common Central European inheritance of the second millennium B.C. when the Greeks themselves inhabited these Danubian countries?

Be this as it may, an event of the greatest importance took place at the moment when Greek penetration in the Getic lands was at its height and when it seemed that the Danube itself would share the fate of the Borysthenes and become a Greek river. Somewhere about the year 280 B.C. the Celts, who had begun their migration towards the east a little before 400 B.C., arrived on the Lower Danube.

Sarmatians, Celts, Germans, Dacians, Thracians fought incessantly against each other or else against the Greeks, victory falling now to the one,

now to the other. From the middle of the second
century onwards, they also fought against the
Romans. The constant turmoil of this barbarian
world profoundly disturbed conditions in the
Danube valley. The sea was infested by pirates.
Getae and Thracians kept attacking the colonies
of the Pontic Greeks. Whether it be at Istria,
Tomi, Callatis, Dionysopolis, Mesambria, Apollonia or Olbia, the inscriptions of the last three
centuries B.C. are full of accounts of wars and
invasions.

In spite of all these trials, however, the
activity of the Greek cities and their economic
relations with the interior continued uninterruptedly. We have shown this elsewhere so far
as Callatis is concerned and have already re-
viewed the Greek finds of the third to the first
century which have been made far up the Danube
valley. For the present we merely wish to add
a few more examples which are typical of the
relations existing in the second and first centuries
between the Getic (or Thraco-Scythian) suzerains
and the Pontic cities which were under their
protection.

The Istrians thank Aristagoras, amongst others,
for having undertaken diplomatic missions a-
mongst the barbarians. Πρεσβήας τε πολλὰς ὑπὲρ
τῆς πόλεως πρεσβεύσας κατὰ τὸ συμφέρον τοῖς

πολείταις διεπράξατο πρὸς [τοὺς κρατοῦντας] τῆς χώρας καὶ τοῦ ποταμ [οῦ βαρβάρους] (that is to say, the Getae of Burebista).

The Callatians honour the good prince Cotys, son of King Rhoemetalkes, with the eponymous magistrature of their city. An honorary decree of the Dionysiac *thiasos* of Callatis, which has recently been discovered and published is dated: ἐπὶ βασιλέος Κότυος τοῦ ʿΡοιμητάλκα. This is an important addition to what Ovid* had already told us about this philhellenic Thracian prince whose education was so perfect that he even composed poems.

> Carmina testantur; quae, si tua nomina demas,
> Threicium iuvenem composuisse negem.
> Neve sub hoc tractu vates foret unicus Orpheus,
> Bistonis ingenio terra superba tuo est.

Ovid had himself been honoured by the bestowal of the *Agonothesia* of the neighbouring city of Tomi. About the year 12 A.D. he appears to have taken advantage of the presence of his poetic colleague, Cotys, at Callatis, to place himself under his protection, for Cotys' father was a faithful friend and ally of Augustus.

> Haec quoque res aliquid tecum mihi foederis affert;
> Eiusdem sacri cultor uterque sumus:
> Ad vatem vates orantia brachia tendo.

The citizens of Dionysopolis thank Acornion,

---

* Ovid, *ex Ponto*. II, 9, 47 sq.

amongst others, for his diplomatic skill in gaining
the goodwill of Burebista towards their city, and
for having afterwards successfully performed the
mission to Pompey with which the Dacian king
had entrusted him. The inscription says of the
king: νεωστεί τε τοῦ βασιλέως Βυρεβίστα πρώτου
καὶ μεγίστου γεγονότος τῶν ἐπὶ Θράκης βασιλέων
καὶ πᾶσαν τήν τε πέραν τοῦ ποταμοῦ καὶ τὴν ἐπὶ
τάδε κατεισχηκότος.

Probably as early as the second century B.C.
the citizens of Odessus express their gratitude to
Ἕρμειος Ἀσκληπιοδώρου, of Antioch, διατρίβων
παρὰ βασιλεῖ Σκυτῶν Κανίτᾳ, a petty Scythian
ruler over the country lying between Callatis and
Odessus, for always being most helpful to their
merchants when travelling in the kingdom of
Kanites.

At about the same period, or perhaps a little
later, the Mesambrians appear to have rewarded
their benefactor Δεμόντης (?) Δήζου Ἀστάς, a
Thracian of the tribe of the Astae, for his kindness to such of their fellow citizens as travelled
in his dominions.

These friendly relations with the Getic kings
certainly helped the Greek merchants to renew
their activities in the Danube valley and in Dacia
as a whole. Most significant of all, perhaps, is
the fact that Burebista, ruler of the whole region

between the Hercynian forest and the Hylaea of the Borysthenites and overlord of the Black Sea coast from Olbia to Apollonia, should have entrusted an embassy to a Greek of Dionysopolis. Even in its mutilated form we can still read on the inscription of Acornion, son of Dionysios, of a visit of his to Argedava, the capital of Burebista's kingdom, in the days of his father and predecessor. That was doubtless why Acornion, an old friend of the Getic royal house should have been chosen for the important mission with which he was later to be honoured.

Our most recent excavations in the Wallachian plain have indeed brought to light a state of affairs which is not a little surprising. Greek commercial expansion in the basin of the Danube and its tributaries was most extensive precisely during the reign of Burebista and his successors, in the third Dacian La Tène period. Greek remains in the ruins of the Geto-Celtic villages are so numerous that, even as far afield as Bucarest, Ploeşti or Turnu Măgurele, one has the impression of being in the rural territory of some Pontic city such as Istria, Tomi or Odessus.

This conclusion, however, is really a perfectly logical one, for it was not until the days of Burebista that the whole Black Sea coast, from Olbia to Apollonia, acknowledged the sway of the Getae. His friends, living in the Pontic cities, could then move freely, under his protection, as far as Lemberg, Prague or Vienna—to use the modern equivalents. Even after the death of Burebista himself, when the Dacian state was once more divided up into several smaller kingdoms, these favourable conditions did not disappear completely. Both Cotiso, king of Western Dacia, and Dicomes, king of Southern Dacia, remained in close contact with the Greco-Roman World and took an active part in the struggles and political intrigues which followed the assassination of Julius Caesar. Dicomes offered his services to Antony against Octavian, while Brutus had been in a similarly favourable position when preparing his offensive in Thrace. Naturally, the instinct of the Dacians showed them that lack of unity in Roman rule was to their advantage: Cotiso became the enemy of Augustus, just as Burebista had been the adversary of Julius Caesar. These interventions of the Dacians in Thrace (cf. Suet. Caes. 44: *Daci, qui se in Pontum et Thraciam effuderant*) were most profitable to their chieftains and warriors. This doubtless explains the large number of gold coins of Κόσων—bearing the effigy of Brutus and struck by his orders in Thrace in 42 B.C.—which have been found in the castles of the Dacian

princes of Transylvania and, above all, at
Grădiştea Muncelului, one of the capitals of this
period.

Dacia had become an integral part of the
Hellenic world. It had first come into the Greek
orbit somewhere about the year 300 B.C. The
victorious wars of Dromichaites against Lysimachus had been followed by peace and collaboration
with the Greeks. The policy of its rulers had combined with the economic activity of the Pontic
cities to bring the Getic lands up to the Carpathians of Moldavia and the Transylvanian
Alps into the stream of Hellenic cultural development from the third century onwards.

In the mountain lands, however, the situation
was quite different. Greek penetration into what
was later to become the Roman province of
Dacia, with its centre of resistance in Transylvania, was much more superficial than was the
case in Wallachia and Moldavia. Nevertheless
the Greeks did not succeed in supplanting the
Celts either to the north or the south of the
Carpathians. The Celts, as an agricultural people,
were much more closely related to the Dacians
than were the Greeks, who were essentially town
dwellers. The Daco-Getic rural population of
course welcomed the visits of Greek merchants
and gladly purchased the excellent wine, fine

ornaments and beautiful vases which they brought with them. Metal-work and pottery—the two principal industries of a settled people—were however carried on throughout Dacia in the new style and according to the new methods which the Celts had brought with them from the West.

We shall deal with these new tendencies in the next chapter. For the present we must conclude with this fundamental point. Greek civilization, in spite of the extent to which it spread through the country, did not succeed in forming a specific Daco-Hellenic culture in Dacia. Once again, western influences were to predominate, for where the Greeks had failed, the Celts succeeded brilliantly.

Chapter IV

CARPATHO-DANUBIANS AND CELTS

IN the year 335 B.C. Alexander of Macedon crossed the Danube into the territory of the Getae of the Wallachian Plain. Amongst the deputations of neighbouring barbarians, which came to greet him on the banks of that great river, there was also one sent by the Celts of the Adriatic. It is therefore not surprising that the first La Tène period (400 to 300 B.C.) should be represented in Transylvania and also in Wallachia. It is true that the evidence for this merely consists of a few *fibulae*, a war chariot, some sword fragments, and, though this is not quite certain, a fine tomb of the fifth or fourth century.* On

---

* The contents of this Celtic tomb[12], which long remained hidden away in a private collection, may belong to the upper valley of the Mureş. The first man to describe it affirmed that the information at his disposal enabled him to place its origin at Silivaş, near Uioara de Mureş. The fine Celtic helmet of Italic type[13], as well as the other objects found there, would lead us to date this find even earlier than 400 B.C., or, in any case, to the very beginning of our first La Tène period. Unfortunately, however, we are by no means sure of the origin of this discovery. The private collector who acquired it might very well have made a mistake. Indeed, while a discovery such as this would agree perfectly with the fifth century finds made in the county of Borsód, it would be most improbable in Transylvania, for it is only from the fourth century onwards that we can really speak of the Celts of Dacia.

the other hand, however, these were all found very far to the east, in the upper valleys of the Mureş, the Olt and the Prahova.

The Dacians must in any case have known the Celts and their civilization by the fourth century B.C. for the latter had arrived in the Getic mountain country between the March and the Upper Theiss at least a century earlier. Reinecke is certainly right in dating the helmets discovered in the districts of Túrócz (Slovakia)[13] and Borsód (North Hungary) to his La Tène A (500 to 400 B.C.). The sword found at Szendrö (in Borsód) belongs to a type which is common to Bohemia, Southern Germany, Northern France and even England, and its original must be looked for between the Marne and the Middle Rhine. The chariot tombs found in this same Getic country between the March and the Upper Theiss, also point to a western original. It is true that these belong to a slightly later period (say the third century), but they really represent a continuation of a tendency which began in the fourth century and for which the chariot tomb at Prejmer, near Braşov, serves as a useful guide. The contents of the tomb at Silivaş, in the very heart of Transylvania[12], are of fifth-century Rhineland style, though their actual origin remains somewhat doubtful.

This northern wave of the great Celtic migration towards the east does not, however, end in Slovakia and in Northern Roumania. There were Celtic *oppida* at Carrodunum, Maetonium, Vibantavarium and Eractum in Galicia and on the Dniester: and very important Celtic workshops at Munkačevo, in Eastern Slovakia, whose products spread throughout Northern Getia. By the third century at the very latest, Galicia, Moldavia, Bessarabia and a portion of the Ukraine as far east as Olbia, were covered by Celtic tribes.* These had advanced through Southern Germany and then down the river Dniester, driving the Germanic tribes of the Bastarnae and Sciri before them as they went. By the year 200 B.C. these Germanic peoples were well known and already firmly established in Moldavia. It follows that the Teuriscii of Northern Dacia (in the Maramureş country, Galicia and Bucovina), and the Britogalli, Britolagae or Brigolati† of Eastern Dacia (Bessarabia), with their cities of Arrubium, Noviodunum and Aliobrix at the mouths of the Danube, could hardly have established themselves here at a later date than that. Moreover, a careful

* As witness the Galatae mentioned in the inscription of Protogenes.
† Cf. the Latobrigi of Gaul.

examination of the information given by Ptolemy as to the place-names of Northern and Eastern Dacia has led us to identify other names, with more or less certainty, as being either Celtic or, at least, as pointing to the presence of Celts, in districts which were ethnographically Getic. Here are a few examples: the Cotensii of Southern Moldavia adjoining the Britogalli of Southern Bessarabia, correspond to the Celtic Cotini of what is now Czechoslovakia on the one hand, and of Western Hungary on the other. The capital of the Cotensii of Moldavia appears to have been Ramidava. The first part of this word is the Gaulish place-name Ramae, which we find in Provence and in the Celtic kingdom of Tylis in Thrace. The Dacian form 'dava', which means town or site, is quite common both in Dacia and in Thrace, as, for example, *Pulpudeva*, 'the town of Philip'. It thus confirms once more the Getic environment in which the Celtic migrants from Galicia had settled down.

The southern Celtic wave is, of course, much better known. Its first stage is represented by the kingdom of the Scordisci on the Danube, in what is now Serbia; and the second in the kingdom of Tylis on the river Hebrus, in Thrace. These two centres of Celtic civilization only came to maturity in the third century, which is a reason

the more for not expecting to find traces of the
first La Tène period in any very considerable
quantity in any part of South-eastern Europe.

From the fourth century onwards, the Celts
seem to have spread over all the Daco-Thracian
lands, and a Celtic cemetery of the second La
Tène period (Reinecke C) at Apahida, near Cluj,
shows us that they had even settled in Transylvania in very large numbers. Indeed, it is impossible nowadays to doubt that between the
year 400 B.C., when the Celts had already made
their appearance on the Upper Theiss, and 200
B.C., which is the real beginning of the Carpatho-
Danubian La Tène period,* we are merely concerned with sporadic manifestations of this new
civilization in Dacia. As against this, however,
the finds of the latter half of the second (approximately 200–100 B.C.) and of the third La Tène
periods are most common, while the La Tène
villages of Dacia are very numerous indeed. In
addition, the objects which have been found—
and this, of course, applies above all to the
pottery—are so abundant, and the forms of the
older civilization appear so submerged by the
new that, if one judged by first impressions only,

* This later La Tène period is the classic age of Celtic metal
work, both military and civil. Swords of both the second and
the third La Tène periods are found in the tombs of this region.

one might well maintain that Dacia had become completely Celtic. At this point, therefore, we must make a rather more detailed examination of Dacian life itself, as evidenced by the products of popular industrial art, in order to distinguish the old from the new—the Daco-Thracian, or Carpathian influences on the one hand, and the Celtic on the other.

The inhabitants of the Dacian villages of the La Tène period lived in fairly small square houses (of dimensions of approximately six feet by twelve), all crowded together. The walls were constructed either of timber or, if near the Danube, of reeds, held together by rough mortar made of earth and built exactly as in the Neolithic Age. The roofs were either of straw or of reeds, while a ditch and palisade defended the house on its most exposed side. As a general rule, these houses were built on a promontory situated near a river or a lake and easy to defend on the land side. The people burned their dead and buried the ashes either in the neighbourhood of the village or under the actual houses in the village itself. We find very little iron amongst the ruins, but a great deal of charcoal. This suggests that we are dealing with a wood, rather than an iron, age. The furniture, chariots and ploughs, together with many other implements

8-2

of peasant life, were made of wood. Even the pots were often of the same material, without mentioning barrels and boats, or the timber houses of the mountainous districts. The remains of pottery in the Celtic style are found side by side with those which continue the old local tradition coming down from the Neolithic Age. In the Wallachian Plain we also find large numbers of fragments of vases of Greek origin, and above all, those of Thasos, Rhodes, Cnidos, or the Pontic settlements. There is no interruption in the layers of successive civilizations, but there is a certain amount of inter-relationship. Thus we find a funeral urn of the old local type side by side with Celtic or Greek goblets and Egyptian glass.

The villages are very small and hardly cover more than from three and a half to five acres. The number of dwellings cannot have been more than a hundred or so. It would be out of place to speak of streets, for all we find are narrow and irregular passages between the houses. In the Wallachian Plain, stores of grain, together with seeds of agricultural and textile plants, have frequently been unearthed. These were preserved in holes in shape like a *dolium*, dug out of the ground under the houses. These stores, moreover, were recognized by classical authors as characteristic of Thracia, and their name of *sirus* (Varro, *de Re Rustica*, I,

57) appears to be of Thracian origin. They contained wheat, flax, hemp and millet, products which appear to have been those most familiar in the Daco-Getic plain amongst the contemporaries of Alexander the Great and of his successors.

The large number of Greek vases—whether *amphorae* with stamped handles, Delian goblets, or Attic *cantharoi*—which have been found almost everywhere in the Dacian villages to the south and east of the Carpathians, help us to date the native and Celtic products with very considerable accuracy. We will speak later of the finds of coins. Their number is extremely small in the actual sites, most of them being found in treasures hidden in solitary places.

So far as we know at present, Greek pottery was almost entirely absent from the Transylvanian villages of the La Tène period. Greek coins, on the other hand, are quite as numerous as the Roman money which makes its appearance in the last three centuries before Christ.

But for the finds made in the mountain fortresses of the Dacian princes, which are scattered throughout the Carpathian range from Czechoslovakia to Southern Transylvania, one would never have suspected the splendour and the vigour of Dacian life in the second Iron Age. Although research actually began about a century ago, it is only some three or four years since serious excavations have really been carried out, and even they are still in the initial stages. Nevertheless, the two series of finds made at Costeşti by the Roumanians and the soundings made long since by the Hungarians at Grădiştea Muncelului and at Piatra Roşie enable us, even now, to form a clear idea as to the sites, the plans, the general structure and the age of these Dacian fortresses of the Carpathians.

The description given by Tacitus (*Annals* IV, 46–51) of the fortresses, or rather the fortified mountains, of Balkan Thrace, finds an exact equivalent in Dio Cassius (LXVIII, 9, 3) when he speaks of the wars of Trajan against the Dacians —for these fortified mountains were also stormed by the Romans. The mountain fortresses of Southwest Transylvania provide us with a perfect example of this: 'montem occupat, angustum et aequali dorso continuum usque ad proximum castellum'. They are like a series of towers with concentric terraces rising up to the summit, where the dwelling of the prince himself was situated. This latter comprises one or more square towers, with walls of as much as nine feet in thickness. The terraces, which must have called for the application of an enormous amount of labour to the rocky massif, are themselves protected on the outer side by palisaded earthworks. The fortress itself is defended by a surrounding wall, of the height of the central terrace, with fairly broad square towers in the main angles. It is constructed of large square blocks of limestone brought from quarries, which were frequently some considerable distance away. This fact gives us some indication of the wealth and power of the princes. The blocks are not held together by metal clamps, in the Greek style, nor by mortar, as in later Roman times, but are kept in place by large wooden beams. This is, of course, the principle of the so-called *murus gallicus*, which was so well known in Gaul and elsewhere in Celtic Europe. In these walls of the Dacian fortresses, however, it is only the foundations which are of stone. The superstructure is of sun-dried bricks as was the case during the archaic period in Greece and in the East. We also find the *appareil à crochet*, as in the Dipylon at Athens. This was known in Provence,* but was most common amongst the Ligurians.

In Dacia, therefore, we find a variation of the *murus gallicus* unknown in the West, and it is very interesting to observe that Trajan's column only gives a very vague reproduction of the

* Cf. Déchelette, *Manuel*, II, 8, p. 998.

actual Dacian method of building in stone and in wood. The impression is, indeed, almost a false one, since, although with certain reservations, it represents the Western Celtic rather than the Daco-Getic system of construction. The similarity in style between the Dacian mountain fortresses to the east of Sarmizegetusa and the so-called 'Goddess Mountain' near Potaissa is so complete that we are forced to the conclusion that this form of construction must have been general throughout the whole of Dacia. We shall consider the age of these Dacian fortresses when we come to speak of Getic religion. For the moment, it will suffice to point out that the fact that they belong to the recent La Tène period is trebly confirmed: in the first place, by fragments of pottery belonging to the third La Tène and by Celtic bronzes of the same period; secondly, by Greek coins of the Black Sea towns of Istria and Mesambria; and, finally, by Celtic coins of the Eravisci of Pannonia.

The strategic position of these Dacian fortresses made them admirable centres for the accumulation of booty by warlike chieftains. They are most numerous in the iron-working region of Transylvania. The anvils, slag and ironware which have been found, well characterize the industrial activity of the period. Small goldsmith's anvils

and famous treasures of gold coins, like those of
Lysimachus and of Koson, have also been discovered. These all point to the political pomp and
great material prosperity of the princes who
reigned here. When we remember that the limestone and the slabs with which the castle at
Grădiştea Muncelului was built and decorated
had all to be brought from a great distance and
raised up to the summit of a mountain some 4000
feet in height, in the face of very great labour
difficulties and unheard-of dangers, it will be
clear that the name of the Getic king Burebista
should stand out above all others. His period was
precisely that of the fine Dacian La Tène III, and
only his power and his wealth can adequately
account for the monumental greatness of an
effort of which even the Romans themselves
would scarcely have been capable.

Let us turn next to the iron industry of Dacia
and examine the principal industrial forms which
characterize the local La Tène period and stand
out as a perfectly well-defined and independent
type of the second Iron Age in Europe. The important workshops at Lovácska and Gallishegy
near Munkačevo are situated in the Getic territory
of the Northern Carpathians. They worked almost
exclusively for the Northern Dacians, while those
at Cudgir, Sebeşel and Grădiştea Muncelului

provided arms and implements for the Dacians of Southern Transylvania. It is not improbable that the iron industry of the Scordisci provided the inhabitants of the Banat and of Little Wallachia with tools and weapons in the Illyro-Celtic style. Indeed, the axes, knives, swords and lances of South-eastern Dacia frequently correspond with those of Illyria, and even with those so far afield as Italy, as we shall show later on. There are also instances, moreover, of the reverse process of Daco-Getic influence in Italy.

The axe is the classic example both of weapon and of tool in pre- and proto-historic days. It is strange, therefore, that one of the most typical forms of the La Tène period in Dacia, the *cateia*, should not as yet have received a satisfactory explanation[15]. While much has been said about Germanic and Merovingian derived forms, little or nothing has been heard about the earlier, more original, and hence, more important bronze, copper or gold axes, in the Carpathian style, which were especially common in the last period of the Transylvanian Bronze Age. Another type, which is quite common in Dacia as in all countries to the east of the Alps, is the heavy iron axe, derived from the socketed axe of the Bronze Age. The knives are also closely related to those of the later Bronze Age, but neither these nor the new form of pruning-hook, which is typical of the second Iron Age, can be regarded as specifically Dacian. They are found everywhere, as is also the case with the scythes, plough-shares, hammers and chisels. On the other hand, the knife with a handle in the middle and a blade at each end, like that found at Vârşeţ, is characteristic for the Illyrian regions: while scythe-shaped swords are absolutely unknown in the Celtic world of the Danube, the Alps and the West.

Trajan's column, which reproduces Dacian weapons, pays particular attention to the swords and curved daggers, examples of which may still be seen in some of our museums. These weapons are probably closely related to the Thracian *sicae* on the one hand, and to the Persian yataghans—as, for example, the Persian's sword on a Pergamene bas-relief in the museum at Naples—on the other. They have nothing to do with Illyrian swords, nor with those of Greco-Italic type such as we find in Attica or in Picenum. The enormous Sarmato-Bastarnian yataghans, which are depicted on the Adamclissi monument, are the 'gladii quos praelongos utraque manu regunt' of which Tacitus speaks (*Hist.* I, 79). Their form is almost identical with that of the Dacian yataghans, though they are infinitely larger and heavier. The iron lances are of quite a common type and are found in very many sizes.

We must conclude, therefore, that, in spite of Celtic infiltrations in Dacia and in spite, also, of the very full knowledge of Celtic civilization which they had acquired, the Getae never completely gave up the local type of weapons in favour of the new models. Celtic swords were quite well known in Dacia, but yataghans were nevertheless used in preference to them.

More complicated still is the question of the Dacian standard[14], on account of the very various elements which enter into it. The Dacian dragon is really a wolf's head drawn out into the form of a large serpent. The wolf was quite a favourite animal pattern, as we see, for example, from the ornamental decorations of Scythian bronze mirror-handles. It does not, however, appear in the standard in its realistic form of repose, but like a fantastic monster in a posture of attack, with its mouth wide open. Examples of this design may be found in the ornamentation of a Scythian sword hilt from Dobolii de Jos, in South-eastern Transylvania (supra, p. 41); in the gold *fibulae* from Mikhalkovo and Dálj (supra, p. 61); in the terra-cotta vase found at Pashaköi (Bulgaria); or again, in engraved and carved bronze objects of the first Iron Age from the

Caucasus region. In each case this head reminds us of that of the Assyro-Babylonian demon Tiamat, or of the Hittite monsters. It served as a standard for the Dacians of the La Tène period and its origin must clearly be sought in the art of Asia Minor sometime during the second millennium B.C. The head itself, however, is attached to a large serpent. This combination is seen on innumerable votive tablets representing the so-called Thracian heroes, *Cabiri*, or *Dioscuri*, or again, according to the latest theory of Rostovtseff, those 'Danubian knights', half Thracian, half Iranian, who were closely associated with the cult of Mithras. This religious association of the dragon with the wolf or the lion is found about the year 1120, on a *stela* of Nebuchadnezzar the First, where, in the fourth quarter, we find an exact representation of the symbol of the Dacian dragon. As was the case with the decorative design of the griffin, which first came from Mesopotamia to Crete in the second millennium, and then, about the year 1000 B.C., was passed on to Central Asia on the one hand, and to Greece, Italy and Gaul on the other, so also this dragon *motif* appears to have become quite familiar in Central Asia and in Europe by the first Iron Age. The standard, which was later called *draco* and served as a military ensign in the armies of the

Roman Empire, must therefore have existed simultaneously amongst the Asiatic Iranians and the Cimmero-Iranians of Europe as early as the first Iron Age. With the Dacians of the La Tène period, it is an element of eastern character and of Iranian type. Amongst the Romans, on the other hand, it would seem to be a Thraco-Getic element which spread throughout the army, thanks to the worshippers of the horsemen gods, whose standard was the *draco* long before the *draco* itself was officially adopted as a Roman ensign. The relief of the Danubian gods actually found at Terracina may well serve as the classic example.

The Dacian war trumpet, as shown on Trajan's column[14], is identical with the Gaulish *carnyx*.* Nothing is more natural, when we bear in mind the zoomorphic style of the *carnyx*. This is closely connected with other and analogous examples from the Dacian La Tène period, as, for instance, the dragon standards on the one hand, and the necklaces, bracelets and rings, with heads of serpents and even of dragons, on the other.

Here, then, we have three elements in the Dacian La Tène period which are definitely southern or even oriental. These are the wall of sun-dried brick, the yataghan and the standard. All three flourished in the midst of a Getic civili-

* Cf. Déchelette, *Manuel*, II, 3, p. 1174.

zation, which was very profoundly influenced by
Celtic elements, both in the iron industry and in
terra-cotta work. But there is still more than all
this. We cannot do more than mention in passing
the toilet utensils discovered in the tombs, or
the clothes of the people, as shown on Roman
monuments. These are not sufficiently typical to
warrant our drawing any definite conclusions.
We must, however, say something of the ornaments, necklaces, bracelets, *fibulae*, and so on,
as an analysis of these from the stylistic point of
view establishes their geographic and ethnographic origin.

In the Bronze Age in Dacia and even in the
first Iron Age gold was used in large quantities
for ornamental purposes. The Dacian La Tène
period, on the other hand, is characterized by an
almost complete absence of gold in the treasures
hidden away during the wars of the period and
by the predominance of silver in its place. This
feature is also apparent in Italy in the same period
(the second and, above all, the third La Tène).
Almost all the Western La Tène forms which have
been noted and commented on by Joseph Déchelette in his classic *Manuel* are also found in
Dacia, though with certain characteristic points
of difference. The Daco-Getae do not appear to
have had any of the fine enamelled chains with

red inlaid work which are, however, found both in Hungary and in Celtic Bohemia. On the other hand, Dacia provides us with a type of ornamental silver chain with curious pendants in the form of small studs, daggers or twisted threads. Up to the present, nothing has been found to correspond with the sumptuous gold necklaces, bracelets and rings richly decorated in the form of a diadem— with figures and geometric patterns derived from Greek originals—which have been met with on the Middle Rhine and on the Garonne, and even at Herczeg Marok in the Baranya district in Hungary. In Dacia itself, silver necklaces, bracelets and rings of spiral form, with serpent heads at both ends, are the typical products of the third La Tène period. There thus appear to be two principal forms. In Italy, Dacia and Dalmatia we find spiral bracelets with serpent heads, made sometimes of gold, though more frequently of silver. In Pannonia, Bohemia and Bavaria, on the other hand, the same objects are found, but in the Rhineland style. It cannot then be a mere coincidence that the same war axes with sockets parallel to the cutting edge and flattened broadly near the handle, and the same types of ornament should be found in Dacia as in Northern and Eastern Italy, as at Ornavasso, for instance, or at Montefortino.

It should not be supposed, however, that there was no connection between the Celtic peoples of the North-east Danubian region—Bavaria, Bohemia and Moravia—and those of Dacia. Amongst both we find thick-stemmed bracelets decorated with projecting curvilinear patterns, while the bronze bracelets with large hollow hemispheres, which are so common in the countries lying between Switzerland and Moravia, are also very numerous in Northern Dacia. These types, however, are absent in Southern Dacia, where the general style approximates much more closely to that of Dalmatia and Italy. The two principal waves of Celtic migration—the northern, which penetrated as far as the Ukraine, and the southern, which ended in Asia Minor—thus appear to have been quite distinct from one another in the influence they exercised on the models and methods of Daco-Getic industrial art during the La Tène period.

Dacian civilization, however, formed too organic a whole for us to divide it up definitely according to the regions of foreign influence. Thus, silver chains with sword-shaped pendants, and large spiral bracelets with serpents' heads, which are so characteristic of the southern districts, are by no means absent from Northern Dacia. So far is this from being the case, that it seems quite possible that the serpent-head spiral bracelets of the third and fourth centuries A.D. discovered in Germany, Scandinavia, and even in Finland, find their prototype, not amongst the Goths of South Russia, where this exact type of bracelet was never really found, but rather in Dacia, where the models of the third La Tène period sometimes appear as absolutely identical with those from the Germanic North.

The pottery of the La Tène period confirms the complete unity of style and civilization in Dacia at this time in a most striking manner. Vases which are evidently of northern origin, like those of Bavaria or Bohemia, have actually been found in Wallachia. Greek penetration, moreover, although very important in the country lying to the east and to the south of the Carpathians, failed to establish Hellenic domination in the traditions of local workmanship. These remained, indeed, under Celtic and not under Greek influence throughout the whole of Dacia. The Celts first introduced the potter's wheel, which had never previously been used by the Carpatho-Danubian peoples. The old style of handicraft, however, still remained and vases of archaic type, reminiscent of Neolithic times, are very numerous in the villages of the La Tène period.

Celtic vases—urns, bowls, cups, plates, basins,

high-standing pedestal-dishes, pitchers, and so on—are extremely numerous. The ware is almost always grey or brown, but sometimes even black or reddish, of fine texture and of very beautiful shapes. In spite of the enormous quantity of this pottery which has been discovered in sites of the third La Tène period in Dacia, it appears nevertheless to have been a foreign product, imported through commercial channels. An examination of the types shows that this finer quality pottery must have come from more northerly Celtic lands. Side by side with these, however, we find a very large number of La Tène vases made locally by the natives themselves. It is very curious to see that these Getic potters, although thoroughly conversant both with the western and the Hellenistic modes of preparation of fine grey earth, nevertheless frequently made these vases by hand, giving them forms essentially rustic and primitive, and reminiscent of Neolithic times.

This local industry continued under the Romans. Moreover the vases found in post-Roman tombs in Dacia bear so close a relationship in type to those of the third La Tène period that we are able to trace the principal features in the development of Daco-Celtic pottery, outside the sphere of purely Roman influences, from the Getae of the time of Burebista right down to the

Goths, the Gepidae, and the Avars of the early
Middle Ages. The only possible explanation is
that the natives, who remained uninterruptedly
in these regions, must have transmitted these
forms from generation to generation.

Illyrian influence is also seen in the Dacian
pottery of the La Tène period. The large bell-
shaped urns made of reddish earth, of the Donja
Dolina type, are however relatively rare. It is
true that they have been found in the valley of
the Mureş and also in that of the Danube, side
by side with metal work which recalls the Late
Hallstatt style of Dalmatia, a country which
never really adopted truly La Tène forms. They
would seem, therefore, to point to more ancient
influences and to the presence of Illyrian ethnic
elements as far as the western frontier of Dacia.
In the case of the high-standing pedestal dishes,
two distinct influences appear to have made themselves felt. On the one hand, the Celts re-intro-
duced elements from the North-west, reminiscent
of the imitations of metal vases of the older
Hallstatt or Alpine civilizations. On the other,
we find vases with high pedestals and turn-down
rims approximating to the Italic type, which
must have come by way of Illyria, and, very
probably, without any direct connection with the
Celts of the South-west.

Southern Greek *amphorae*, Delian goblets, and *cantharoi*, perhaps Attic, of the same late Hellenistic period, are frequently found in the Getic sites of the Wallachian Plain. They were brought up the Danube and its tributaries for quite a considerable distance into the Transylvanian Alps. Transylvania itself, however, has not as yet provided us with a single example of this eastern work. Nevertheless there is no reason for supposing that the peoples of Central and Northern Dacia had not seen any Hellenistic pottery, since this product made its way much further north than Transylvania. We may add that coloured glass vases, and more especially those in cobalt blue, which is typical of the third La Tène period, were also imported into the Wallachian plains.

At this point let us pause for a moment to consider the industrial and commercial activity of Dacia in La Tène times.

When we bear in mind the large number of tools and weapons of the second Iron Age which have been found in Dacia—amongst which the daggers and the curved swords are of a type not forged anywhere else—it seems probable that the iron mines were exploited much more thoroughly than the few finds of forges, slag, anvils and hammers would seem to suggest. On the other hand, it is no less probable that the Celts were the instructors of the Getae in this type of working in metal. Indeed, most of the iron tools forged in Dacia are not derived from the corresponding forms of the last period of the Getic Bronze Age, but are absolutely identical with those found in the West. Ploughshares, scythes, sickles, pruning-hooks, and so forth are the same both amongst the Celts and the Dacians. As also in Western Europe, the principal metal-working centres were certainly the *castellieri* of the high mountains. The proximity of the iron mines to the fortresses of South-eastern Transylvania was certainly not accidental. The finds of silver ore and jewellers' tools made in these same Dacian fortresses show that the beautiful silver ornaments—conceived in what is on the whole a local style—which have been found in the tombs, together with the hidden deposits of the third Getic La Tène period, must have been made on the spot. It is, of course, quite true that the large number of Thasian and Macedonian silver coins provided excellent raw material for the Dacian jewellers. Nevertheless, Dacian coins of the local type would alone have used up all the foreign silver, if the mines of the country itself had not made good the deficit. An equally helpful suggestion is given us by the ancient authors who wrote of the treasure of Decebalus which fell into the hands of Trajan. So much gold—whether in the form of specie or, as was more frequently the case, in vases and ornaments—could hardly have been obtained solely as a result of the invasions and foreign wars of Burebista and his successors. Some must also have been acquired thanks to hard work in the placer mines and the gold-bearing river sands which are so numerous in Dacia.

It is nevertheless difficult to free oneself from the direct impression, obtained both from discoveries made *in situ* and from exhibits in the museums, that in Dacia, as in Gaul, gold was not the leading precious metal in the La Tène period as it had been in the Bronze Age. Even in a gold-producing country like Dacia, silver was much more common than gold. The Dacians themselves, who learnt from the Celts, amongst many other things, the art of coining money, never minted any gold coins. Their concave tetradrachms are very broad and thin and are imitated either from the silver staters of Philip II and the tetra-drachms of Alexander the Great, or else from the Thasian tetradrachms. They contain a large amount of alloy, bronze, for instance, rising to as much as 55 per cent., while there is hardly 34 per cent. of silver in the case of the find at Petelea in the upper valley of the Mureş. There were, however, no corresponding gold coins. Forrer's hypothesis* that the Dacians also minted gold coins seems to me to be completely arbitrary. All the reasons he adduces in support of his thesis can also be used to prove the contrary: that is to say, that these coins were Celtic and not Dacian. Similarly, the alleged Dacian bronze and copper coins are plainly Celtic 'intruded' coins, which are quite common in the region of the Lower Danube.

The number of Dacian imitations of Macedonian and Thasian tetradrachms is very large. In comparison, however, with genuine foreign coins, both Greek, which we find from the fourth century onwards, and Roman, which made their appearance towards the end of the third century and spread throughout Dacia as trade increased, the rôle of these barbarian imitations is very limited. They do not seem to have had more than a very restricted and possibly compulsory, local circulation, since everybody preferred the sound money of the Greeks and the Romans.

The number of Celtic coins—and in this connection we are thinking above all of their characteristic gold issues, the so-called '*Regenbogenschüsselchen*' and the imitations of Roman

* R. Forrer, *Keltische Numismatik der Rhein- und Donaulande* (Strassburg, 1908), p. 206 sqq.

denarii—is very limited in Dacia. As they were both of them peoples living on a similar cultural level, the Dacians and the Celts had very few commercial dealings with one another on a money basis. It is true that we find coins both of the Eravisci and of Istria and Mesambria side by side in the fortress of a Dacian prince at Costeşti. Nevertheless, this merely gives us an indication of the possibilities of commerce existing in Dacia in both directions and is no evidence of the intensity of these commercial relationships. The main commercial channels of Dacia were controlled neither by the Greeks of the Black Sea, nor by the Celts of Pannonia, but by the big exporters of wine and oil in Greece proper and in Macedonia, and, later by Italian merchants and Greeks from the Adriatic. The coins we chiefly find throughout Dacia are, first of all those of the Greeks of the Aegean and, later, those of the Romans, but not the coins of the Pontic Greeks nor those of the Celts of the Middle Danube.

It is only when we bear in mind the enormous number of fragments of Greek *amphorae*—coming mainly from Thasos, Rhodes and Cnidos, but sometimes from other places also—which have been discovered on La Tène sites in Moldavia and Wallachia, and which are sometimes even as numerous as the pottery of Celtic origin, that we realize how intense was Hellenistic penetration in Southern and Eastern Dacia. One almost has the impression of being in the inland possessions of a Greek city of the Black Sea. The fact that we find in Dacia so many Macedonian and Greek silver coins from the fourth century onwards, together with Thasian *amphorae* dating from the same period, proves that the wine, oil, bronze vases, steel weapons, vases in coloured glass, mail ornaments and bronze harness-ornaments which the Greek merchants brought with them did not suffice to pay for their purchases of corn, honey, skins, salt and slaves in this rich country. The Dacians had long had an industrial art of their own, and their ornaments were more valuable and sometimes even more beautiful than corresponding Greek products. The merchants, therefore, had to pay in money as well. The Romans, when they came in large numbers into the Danubian regions, more especially towards the beginning of the second century B.C., also paid in cash for the goods they bought. Treasures of Roman *denarii* of the last two centuries of the republic and of *drachmae* from Apollonia and Dyrrhachium are extremely numerous in Dacia, and the date at which most of these were buried is very significant, a large number of the treasures ending with *denarii* of the year 44 B.C. It is not in the

least difficult to identify the historical event
which was responsible for this. Like Gaul during
the same period, Dacia must have been full of
Italici negotiandi causa consistentes. As soon as
they heard of the expedition which Caesar was
preparing against Burebista they made good their
escape. First of all, however, they buried the
treasure which they could not take with them,
hoping to return with the victorious Roman
armies and find it again.

A statistical review of the hoards found in
Dacia shows that the south-eastern parts of the
country were covered, in the main, by Greek
merchants, while the Romans spread to the west
and to the north. From the first century B.C.,
however, Roman penetration was at once so
powerful and so general that *denarii* of the republic became quite frequent in Wallachia and
even in Moldavia. A late third La Tène site in the
Wallachian Plain, like that at Tinosul on the
river Prahova, actually shows a closer relationship with the Roman market than with the Greek.
Mirrors in white metal and bronze vases which
were either made in Southern Italy or at least in
the South Italian style, and again a sestertius of
Agrippina, combine to bear witness to this change
of front in matters economic and artistic. As to
Transylvania, the bronze vases of Campanian

origin which have already been discovered, lead us to hope much from the results of future excavations.

In spite of the preponderance of these influences from the South, whether Hellenic or Italic, the Dacians nevertheless remain an essentially northern people during this Celtic period. Their industrial art is still geometric in design, even when they adopt decorative patterns with animal heads. Their religion remains aniconic and their supreme god is still the sole master of the clouded sky whom they worship in caves or on high mountain peaks.

From the last period of the Bronze Age onwards, Getic art in Dacia had been fairly continuously under the influence of naturalistic tendencies coming from the Cimmerians, the Scythians and the Ionian Greeks to the east, and from the Veneto-Illyrians to the west. Small bronze animal figures, either in the naïve Scytho-Siberian style or of the more or less strictly geometric Hallstatt type, have been found everywhere in Dacia. A group like that from Năeni in Wallachia, representing Anaïtis riding on a lion between two acolytes (supra, p. 44), or a *rhyton* like that at Poroina near Severin, which represents the Great Goddess, are witnesses to Iranian influences which penetrated into Dacia and established themselves there even in the La Tène period. Nevertheless, the Getae remained faithful to their own geometric style. Even in the second Hallstatt period, the decorative pattern of a dragon head or a serpent was quite common in Dacia, while spiral rings with this ornament at one of the ends, are quite frequent in the art of those days. This pattern was fairly widespread throughout Europe but was very much to the fore in such countries as Scythia and Italy, which had great influence over Dacia precisely during this period. It might have come to our country equally well from the one side as from the other. The actual way in which this pattern was developed in Dacia, however, is so new, while its resemblances to the workmanship and style of other countries are so few—indeed, the only case we know of is the scabbard of a Scythian dagger found in Melgunov's barrow—that these bracelets may well be considered as specifically Dacian products. The animal head, which is in the form of a complete geometric pattern adorned with linear incisions, is continued towards the interior of the spiral by a flattened band decorated externally by a chain of *palmettes* in geometric design and struck in much the same way as a coin. This Dacian type appears to have been adopted later by the Germanic peoples also, through the medium of the neighbouring tribes of the Quadi and the Marcomanni, and even spread as far as Sweden and Finland. The human figure is likewise found in Dacian art of the La Tène period, either in repoussé and then engraved and dotted, as on the silver plate found at Cioara; or else cut and engraved in relief, as in the case of a large Transylvanian *fibula* representing a human mask; or else on pendants or decorative discs. In the main, however, Dacian art remains aniconic.

A critical review of Getic monumental architecture would make this chapter unduly long. The few indications which have already been given about the castles of Central Dacia must suffice in this connection. It may be noted, in passing, that Getic decorative sculpture did not exist, and that the stones, although well squared and polished, never received any plastic ornamentation, with the sole exception of an occasional simple vertical groove in angles of the buildings.

Something must, however, be said about the funeral rites and the religion of the Getae. Ever since Chalcolithic times the inhabitants of Dacia, almost without exception, had practised cremation. They remained so true to this rite that, even in the time of the Romans, when the newcomers buried their dead in *sarcophagi*, either in cemeteries or in isolated tombs, the Dacians

themselves continued to burn their dead and
bury the ashes in funeral urns of archaic form.
The Celts who came to Dacia certainly cremated
their dead from the second La Tène period onwards. We do not, however, possess a single Celtic
tomb which can be definitely ascribed to the first
La Tène period. It is therefore impossible to say
whether the Celts began by resisting this practice.
This the Scythians certainly did, for even those
who actually lived amongst the Getae remained
true to the rite of interment as practised in
Southern Russia. The Celtic tombs of North-
western Dacia contain remains of food dedicated
to the dead, as was customary in Gaul. We find
pigs, chickens and also wild boars so offered up.
Apart from the sacred vases—urns, goblets,
bowls or cups—these tombs contain remains of
the warrior's equipment, such as his weapons, his
ornaments and sometimes, as at Balsa, even the
wheels of his war chariot. Getic tombs, on the
other hand, are strikingly simple. Hardly anything is found either in or near the funeral urn,
while the urn itself is but rarely up-to-date in its
workmanship. It is hand-made, in accordance
with the models of the old Neolithic tradition,
though Greek *amphorae* are sometimes used as
urns. But Getic and Celtic tombs are flat,
whereas Scythian burials are beneath *tumuli*. We

do, however, occasionally find grave mounds under which cremated bodies are interred. At Caşolţ, near Sibiu, for example, there is a large necropolis of barrows, in all of which the bodies have been cremated.

In the fortresses of the Dacian princes of the mountains of South-west Transylvania we find most curious types of construction. They are situated on the lower terraces outside the walls of the citadel, and are of the two following varieties. At Grădiştea Muncelului [16] we find a circle of stone blocks, carefully squared, and forming a sort of *cordon* similar to that encircling the *tumuli* of the Etruscans or the archaic Greeks. They are, however, in double row, the slabs of the outer circle being low and close together, while those of the inner circle are much higher and farther apart. Similar monuments found throughout Central and Southern Europe show us that, in the first Iron Age, these circular rings of stone blocks fixed in the ground were of funerary character. No explanation, however, has as yet been found for these old stone circles, with their slabs some distance apart from one another. Every seventh stone is broader than the others, the general effect suggesting some numerical relationship of a mystic character. Dacia itself, however, does not afford us any other

example of a circular cordon like that at Grădiştea
Muncelului.

Still more enigmatic are the stone alignments
at Costeşti[15]. These, as in the previous case, are
situated on the broad terrace surrounding the
citadel and consist of several lines of very small
drums of limestone little more than a foot in
height. They are exact repetitions of the celebrated megalithic monuments found in Brittany.
Like the circular monuments at Grădiştea Muncelului, however, the alignments at Costeşti
belong to the second Iron Age, and we know of
nothing resembling them in the rest of Europe at
that period. The number of stones would point to
some funeral rite, but nothing definite can as yet
be advanced to explain these constructions. Their
religious character is obvious, but their precise
meaning remains obscure.

Who built these curious constructions? and
who were the lords of the castles which dominated
them? Were they Celts or were they Getae? The
small objects and coins found in them would
suggest that the Celtic hypothesis must be ruled
out. Indeed, as early as about the year 60 B.C.,
Burebista had completely destroyed every independent Celtic organization up to the Alps,
and the fortresses at Grădiştea Muncelului and
Costeşti flourished precisely at that period. It

might, of course, be argued that these circular cordons and alignments are older, and really belong to the fourth century. That was the period of the great Celtic advance which brought these warriors with their war chariots as far as Eastern Transylvania. We, for our part, think this unlikely, in view of the fact that the Celts themselves had long since lost the habit of building in this manner. Pending further excavations, the question must remain an open one.

It has been stated (supra, p. 70) that the supreme deity of the Getae, Zalmoxis, was the ancient Zeus, master of the cloudy˙ sky, the thunder-god. He is not represented in any plastic design. The caves on the mountain tops where he was worshipped have not as yet been identified, nor has his principal sanctuary of Kogaionon, of which Strabo speaks. But this great Uranian god was not the only one worshipped by the Dacians. It is true that the Thracian gods of the Rhodope mountains and Mount Pangaeus have nothing in common with the religion of the Getae, while references to the chthonian, orgiastic beliefs of the Dacians are a mere confusion of modern historical criticism. The existence of the great pre-Indo-European goddess, however, that cruel virgin of the Cimmerians of the Bosphorus, known as Aphrodite Ourania or Royal Artemis, and later, as

Diana Regina, is quite well assured. In our excavations of pre-historic sites, the number of plastic representations of this great goddess, in a sitting posture, is increasing almost every day. In the Danubian Chalcolithic period we find terra-cotta models showing the goddess seated, her acolytes standing, with the throne and the votive table close at hand. Appearance, gesture and costume frequently remind us of Minoan art forms. It is the same seated goddess whom we see appear once again—after the crisis of the chthonian religion during the Bronze Age, with its Indo-European peoples who adored the sky and the sun—on Scythian gold and silver plates. These represent the solar knight, the *Açvin* and the *Dioscuros*, coming to receive the sacred drink from the hands of the goddess. The *rhyton* of Poroina also represents her, as do the innumerable pictorial representations of the Danubian knights and the *patera* of the treasure of Petroasa.

The ancient chthonian beliefs of the natives of the Mediterranean lands were overthrown and, for a moment, totally submerged by the new Uranian religion of the Indo-European conquerors. Slowly, however, they came once more into their own and, in particular, the Mediterranean cult of the goddess mother was destined never again to be overcome.

A careful examination of the forms of civilization in the Dacian La Tène period shows us that, in fact, the history of the Daco-Roman people actually begins as early as the third century B.C., although its earliest origins, at any rate from the ethnographic point of view, go back to the Bronze Age. First the Villanovans and then the Celts, pupils, both of them, of the advanced civilization of the Eastern Mediterranean, bring Hellenic influences to bear upon the Dacians, but in western garb. In this sense, the arrival of the Romans was to afford no new surprise for the Daco-Getae. The proto-history of Dacia is thus the best introduction to the history of Roman influence in the East. Lying, as it did between the Cimmerians, Scythians and Greeks on the one side, and the Italic, Illyrian and Celtic peoples on the other—two worlds profoundly different in mentality and civilization alike—the geographical situation of Dacia as an integral part of Central Europe led, as early as the year 1000 B.C., to a connection with the West rather than with the East. The final result of this could be none other than the Romanization of this eastern land. Its true initiators in this westward movement were the Celts; its best associates were the Illyrians; its greatest masters, the Romans.

Chapter V

THE second century B.C. saw Rome pursuing her path of conquest alike in East and West and gradually imposing her rule on Spain, Africa, Macedonia, and Asia Minor. Yet there was no territorial link between these scattered fragments of empire: Italy proper stopped at the Apennines. Cisalpine Gaul, and the thin strip of Gallic territory between Alps and Pyrenees (called simply Provincia), which was later annexed in order to secure communication by land between Spain and Italy, had each possessed a culture of its own, but these had been submerged by the great La Tène civilization of Celtic Europe. We are apt to forget that even in the first century B.C. when Rome had already occupied Syria, Latin was not too well spoken at Padua, Verona, or Milan. The civilization of Cisalpine Gaul was on a par rather with Celtic Europe than Roman Italy, and the romanized Cisalpines were far more nearly allied in race and spirit to Gauls, Illyrians, or Dacians than to Latins.

Not till the reign of Augustus did Rome essay the conquest of the provinces which stretch north

and east of the Alps up to the Danube, and even
then the conquest was not completed. Pannonia Inferior, Moesia Inferior, and Thrace still
remained outside the system, while Noricum and
Rhaetia preserved their native constitution,
though under a Roman protectorate, for many
years. The first Roman road along the Danube,
between the two legionary camps of Viminacium
(V Macedonica) and Ratiaria (IV Scythica) was
only built by the soldiers of the two legions in
33/34 A.D., and the Danubian frontier was not
organized along its whole length till under
Claudius: at any rate for the Lower Danube we
have no document prior to the letter despatched
by Flavius Sabinus, governor of Moesia from 43
to 49 A.D., to the citizens of Istria, wherein we
gain our first notice of the customs there, τὸ τῆς
κατὰ τὸν Ἴστρον ὄχθης τέλος μέχρι θαλάσσης.

Yet Velleius, scarcely fifteen years after
Augustus, through his legate Tiberius, had conquered the Pannonians, could declare that all
these 'barbari' can understand Latin: 'omnibus
autem Pannoniis non disciplinae tantummodo sed
linguae quoque notitia Romanae; plerisque etiam
litterarum usus et familiaris erat armorum exer-
citatio'. By 52/53 A.D. Moesia was regarded as
sufficiently Roman to have settled upon it more
than 100,000 barbarians from beyond the Danube

CARPATHO-DANUBIANS AND ROMANS 151

'with their wives, their children, their princes or chiefs', who had been captured or received into submission by Plautius Silvanus, and the province began to send 'vast quantities of grain' to Rome to relieve the famine then reigning in Italy. By Vespasian's time the veterans and the Roman civilians settled in the Danubian provinces as far as the Black Sea are legion.

Such a transformation seems miraculous, and there must be some cause which has escaped us, for the history of civilization knows no miracles; a world cannot be completely romanized in less than forty years. Yet after making all qualifications and admitting the existence of a large mass of population (composed of Celtic, Illyrian, and Thracian elements), which had no notion of Latin or of Roman life, one fact remains unshaken—for it is witnessed by the monuments—that Roman towns and villages arose on all sides. By the reign of Nero, and still more by the days of Vespasian, there was a Roman Illyricum; by the second century we find, side by side with the local Illyrian, Celtic, or Thracian place-names, a definite and established system of Latin names (as in the rivers Picusculus or Turgiculus).

The reason is—as proto-history has shown us —that the beginning of Roman penetration (using the word in its cultural sense) into the

Danubian countries must be placed well back in
the second century B.C. We must look for the
vigorous *conventus civium Romanorum negotiandi
causa consistentium* not only in the hellenized
Orient but even more in the barbarian countries,
neighbouring or distant, where Celtic immigration had awakened the people to the need for a
better organized civil life, for comfort and luxury.

As early indeed as 180 B.C. Livy tells of *cives
Romani* and of *socii Latini nominis* who had been
molested and attacked in the Dalmatian kingdom
of Gentius. Caesar mentions the *conventus civium
Romanorum* of Salonae, to which the author of
the *Bellum Alexandrinum* adds: 'Salonas...
oppidum maritimum quod cives Romani fortis-
simi fidelissimique incolebant'. These were the
adventurous spirits who penetrated far into the
interior to exploit the resources of so rich a
territory, and so helped to bring about its rapid
economic development. Both Narona and Lissus
appear in the list of Roman centres which were
active from republican times. More significant
still is the fact that the great route leading north-
east from Italy towards the Danube, with its
important mart, Nauportus, which was the key
of the passes down to the Save, had its own
conventus civium Romanorum long before the
imperial organization of this region. On

Pannonia Velleius furnishes valuable information. At the time of the Pannonian revolt, less than twenty years after the annexation, the Romans found the rebels very well organized, thanks to their knowledge of Roman language and customs: 'itaque hercules nulla umquam natio tam mature consilio belli bellum iunxit ac decreta patravit' (these words would apply equally well to the Dacia of Decebalus and for the same reasons); 'oppressi cives Romani, trucidati negotiatores, magnus vexillariorum numerus ad internecionem ea in regione quae plurimum ab imperatore aberat, caesus', etc. Roman citizens and business men could be found even where there were no troops, as was the case at the time of Caesar's invasion of Gaul. Even before that the land was full of Roman merchants and *negotiatores*, as Cicero tells us (pro Fonteio, 5, 11): 'referta Gallia negotiatorum est, plena civium Romanorum, nemo Gallorum sine cive Romano quicquam gerit, nummus in Gallia nullus sine Romanorum tabulis commovetur'. No danger could frighten these hardy pioneers, and Caesar recounts an expedition that he had to send to guard the direct route from Gaul to Milan across the *Alpes Poeninae*, 'quo magno cum periculo magnisque cum portoriis mercatores ire consuerant'.

We have already tried to prove (see Chap. IV),

by means of the discoveries made in Dacia, that from the second century onward we must reckon with a penetration of Italic elements, and that from the time of Burebista (circa 50 B.C.) Dacia was as full of merchants as Gaul or the Celtic Alps. But we must not think of merchants only when we consider Roman penetration into the Danubian lands: kings and chieftains (Celtic, Illyrian, or Dacian) must have needed plenty of skilled labour to build their strongholds, make their engines of war, or strike their money, usually on the model of the *denarii* of the Roman republic. Even the Celtic coins of Pannonia have legends in *Latin* characters. Lastly, then as now, there were adventurers ready to turn their hand to any task, from diplomatic negotiations to the selling of prisoners-of-war as slaves.

It is likely enough that from the second century onwards Celtic had to yield something of its position as a 'diplomatic language' to Latin, which was already becoming the common speech of Gallia Cisalpina, a region that was the hub of all Italian enterprise towards the Danubian lands. Greek appears to have played little or no part in Central Europe. Though military expeditions towards the Danube for more than a century (168–29 B.C.) made Macedonia their base, cultural penetration came for the most part direct from Italy across the Adriatic and Dalmatia or over the Julian Alps and down the Save valley.

On this point coin-hoards and other finds in Dacia offer us definite testimony. By the side of hundreds of Roman *denarii* of the Republic, discovered mostly in the western and southern regions, though also in Moldavia, we find a quantity of *drachmae* of Apollonia and Dyrrhachium, and the mode of their circulation is perfectly clear. The Greeks of these two important towns of the Southern Adriatic travelled either from Macedonia by the north-western route (through Paeonia and Dardania, and down the Margus and Timacus) or else by the route through Dalmatia, down the Drinus to its confluence with the Save and then down that river. These coins of Apollonia and of Dyrrhachium are nearly always discovered in the same hoards as the Roman *denarii*: the Italians and the Greeks of Illyria were making common cause, but ever since the Roman conquest of Dalmatia these two Greek towns were almost Italic themselves. Bronze pieces of Corcyra, or copper coins of Scodra, Issa, and the Molossi of Epirus, coins of Pharos, or even of Panormus or Valentia (Hipponium), round off the picture of Italic penetration into pre-Roman Dacia by way of Dalmatia, and their evidence is still further confirmed by industrial products of Southern Italy, such as mirrors and bronze vessels, which are also found there.

Macedonia was not, indeed, a rich country; the mines of Pangaeus no longer made it so desirable; but once involved in the Balkans the Romans found it difficult to withdraw. Illyrians, Celts, Scordisci, Dacians, Bastarnae, all invaded the province singly or in combination. The Romans were compelled to take an ever-increasing interest in the rich Danubian lands, and especially in Dacia, which became the richest and most powerful of all. From the end of the second century they had begun to regard it as a breeding ground for invasions: 'Minucius Rufus imperator a Scordiscis Dacisque premebatur, quibus impar erat numero', says Frontinus (Strateg. II, 4, 3) and Florus (I, 39, 6) recounts under the events of the year 74, à propos of the expedition of C. Scribonius Curio, 'Dacia tenus venit, sed tenebras saltuum expavit'. By this time Burebista had started on his career of conquest: as Strabo says, 'in a few years he founded a vast empire, imposing Getic rule upon almost all his neighbours; he became a menace to the Romans too, seeing that he used to cross the Danube without fear and ravage Thrace as far as Macedonia and Illyria; the Celts, who had combined with the Thracians and Illyrians, were annihilated, and the Boii, under their king Critasirus, and the Taurisci were subdued'. In addition, in order to consolidate the hold he had secured over these territories, he was prepared to exercise a subtle diplomacy: he offered Pompey his support against Caesar: his ambassador, a Greek, Acornion of Dionysopolis, was actually received in audience by Pompey in 48 B.C. near Heraclea Lyncestis: 'πρός τε Γναῖον Πομπήϊον Γναίου υἱὸν αὐτοκράτορα 'Ρωμαῖον ἀποσταλεὶς ὑπὸ βασιλέως Βυραβείστα πρεσβευτὴς καὶ συντυχὼν αὐτῷ τῆς Μακεδονίας ἐν τῷ περὶ 'Ηράκληαν τὴν ἐπὶ τοῦ Λύγκου οὐ μόνον τοὺς ὑπὲρ τοῦ βασιλέως χρηματισμοὺς διέθετο τὴν εὐνοίαν τὴν 'Ρωμαίων παραγόμενος τῷ βασιλεῖ, ἀλλὰ κτλ' (Dittenberger Syll. 3, 762). The significance of this act of Burebista was not lost on Caesar: even after his defeat of Pompey he did not give up the idea of making war on the Dacians, and had indeed begun the concentration of troops in the East when he was assassinated in 44 B.C. Fortunately for Rome Burebista himself was murdered and the conspirators parcelled out among themselves the great empire he had founded.

But his policy remained. The Dacians continued to interfere in the civil wars of Rome, and even took sides, some led by Cotiso for Octavian, some led by Dicomes for Antony. For a moment, indeed, it looked as though the king of Western Dacia, Cotiso, would strengthen an alliance with Octavian by the ties of marriage: his daughter was to marry the emperor, and Augustus' daughter Julia was to become the wife of the Dacian king. But the questions at issue were too vast and the Dacians too near to Italy to allow of so facile a settlement. Burebista's conquest of Pannonia and of the lands of the Taurisci, Scordisci, and Triballi, meant that Dacian horsemen could in a few days reach the shores not only of the Aegean or Adriatic but even descend upon Italian territory itself.

So clear a menace naturally changed the direction of the Roman counter offensive. Attacks began to be made from the west down the Save valley as well as from Macedonia, and Siscia became the headquarters for the war against the Dacians. But neither the aggressive policy of Augustus and of his legates (as seen in the campaigns of Crassus from the south, Catus from the south-west, Lentulus from the south and south-west, Tiberius from the west, and Vinicius from the north-west), nor the cautious defensive of Tiberius (which consisted in holding the fortified Danube line), did much to improve the situation. In the end Domitian and after him Trajan had to organize campaigns on a large scale before the Dacian power could be finally checked.

Between the efforts of Minucius Rufus and the wars of Trajan against the Dacians lay two whole centuries of warfare, and after so long a training there was not a Dacian who did not appreciate what Rome was. When Domitian agreed to make peace with Decebalus, before he had decisively beaten him, the Dacian chief (in his rôle of client king) asked not only for subsidies from the Empire, but for engineers and workmen, armourers and workers in metal. It was but a continuation of the policy that, more than a century before, a Burebista or Cotiso must have pursued, for the strongholds of the La Tène period in Dacia also show traces of Roman technique, at any rate in the more recent parts of their building and construction and in their artistic monuments. Before the battle of Tapae (in the first campaign of Trajan) a Dacian tribe, the Buri, actually sent a letter in Latin to the emperor, from themselves and from the other barbarian allies, advising him not to make war. By this time there existed in Dacia, as in Pannonia a hundred years before, a sufficient number of natives who understood the language, besides a large Roman element in the Dacian service itself, for letters to be written in Latin.

It will be enough, therefore, to emphasize again the close connection, both in material and spiritual life, which had existed between Italians and Dacians. Though the Celts had been intermediaries at first, direct contact was soon established and had lasted for some centuries before Trajan. Let us now pass on to discuss the situation that resulted from the complete and definitive settlement of the Romans in the basin of the Lower Danube, in the Carpathians as well as in the Balkans.

The first region properly occupied by them, first with one legion, circa 15 A.D., and then with two, circa 23 A.D., was Moesia (afterwards called Moesia Superior), that portion of the Danube which faced the Dacians of the mountains. This country had been previously administered (under the auspices of the governor of Macedonia) by a *praefectus civitatium Moesiae et Triballiae*, and was inhabited by a population composed of Thracian, Illyrian and Celtic elements; they were fond of war and had scarcely emerged out of the savage state, engaging, for the most part, in stock-raising rather than in agriculture proper. Only on the very bank of the Danube itself and in the valley of the Margus or of the Timacus could there be any question of bringing into being prosperous urban life on Roman lines. Here, as in Dalmatia, the Romans laid down the boundaries between the *civitates* of the different tribes, and handed over to the prefects sent to those *civitates* the administration of public business and jurisdiction.

Yet even so Romanization did not progress very fast, and this led the Flavian emperors to force the pace somewhat by founding a military colony at Scupi. It was apparently restored by Hadrian, who gave it his name also, yet the whole region must have remained strongly Thracian. *Zeus Zberturdus* was the god worshipped there, and the Bessi were a strong element. In a list of veterans of the Legio VII Claudia dating from 195 A.D. we come across a whole series of legionaries from Scupi bearing names such as *Bithus*, *Mestula*, *Sausa*, or *Daizo*; but Illyrian names such as *Dassius* (and after all it is not certain that this is an exclusively Illyrian name) are rare.

Under Trajan Ratiaria became a colony, but that did not prevent it remaining a very important Thracian centre. In the list of veterans just cited we find such names as *Dolens*, *Stambon*, *Drigissa*, *Thamarcus*, *Thithus*, *Bithus* (very common in Moesia Superior), *Sinna* and *Curta*. Progress continues slowly: under Hadrian the urban centre of Viminacium was raised to the dignity of a *municipium*, and so was Margum under the Antonines; we do not know at what date Singidunum became a *municipium*, but it was certainly not a *colonia* till after the reign of Septimius Severus. By 169 A.D. we find a large number of Romans enrolled in the Legio VII Claudia, and the following towns contributing recruits (the list is not complete)—Pautalia, Sarmizegetusa, Sirmium, Ratiaria, Scupi, Mursa, Salonae, Nicopolis, Thessalonica, Iader, Viminacium, Heraclea, Trimontium, Philippi, and Romula, among others, but Ratiaria and Scupi are at the head. These recruits are Thracians or Illyrians more or less romanized in their respective homes (for the most part they come from the rural territories of these Roman towns), and during their military service (which in this instance lasted twenty-seven years!) they picked up much more than mere military training. For Latin was the language of the legion, and (to give an example) Mucatra, the *praepositus* in charge of the making of bricks and tiles for the legion at Viminacium, must stamp his mark on them in Latin, however much he may still have talked in Thracian with his fellow-soldiers or with civilians. Even in 270 the names of these latter at Viminacium are still Thracian: *Cutia, Cutius, Bessio,* etc. Their religion too remained Thracian. At Singidunum we meet a *collegium* of Romano-Thracian 'collitores' of the Deus Heron: at Naissus we have a dedication (from the year 223) to *Iupiter Optimus Maximus*

Paternus Aepilofius ('Επιλόφιος), who is no other than *Zalmoxis* or *Gebeleizis*, worshipped on lonely peaks: at Timacum Minus we find a dedication to *Hercules Naisates*, which reminds us of the innumerable Thracian dedications to gods whose titles are taken from local place-names, such as the *Sanctus Casebonus* in Moesia who is merely the god of the district Κασιβόνων. Even official dedications corresponded to Thracian beliefs; for instance, at the entrance to the copper mines of Rudnik (north-east of Kragujevatz), which the Romans exploited, a ruined temple of Terra Mater was restored in the name of Septimius Severus; at Ratiaria the goddess is called *Proserpina*, as the wife of *Dis Pater*; at Singidunum, where she is called *Dea Orcia*, the dedication was made in honour of Diocletian and Maximus by the *IIviri* of the *splendidissima colonia*, and these magistrates bore the name of *Cutia* and *Soso* respectively. Yet in reality this goddess, though masked as *Ceres*, *Diana*, or *Nemesis*, is always the local great goddess, whose most common name among the Thracians of the Danube was that of *Diana Regina*, just as seven centuries before Herodotus had likened her to Ἄρτεμις Βασιληίη.

Thus at the beginning of the third century of our era Moesia Superior was still strongly

Thracian. Yet efforts were made to keep in contact with Rome and Roman culture: there is something rather touching in an inscription such as that from Timacum Minus, which tells how a Roman knight from that district sent his young son to Rome, probably to complete his studies there, but the poor boy *vitam insidiis in sacra urbe finivit.* Yet Latin as spoken in Moesia was adapted to local pronunciation: we find *cusit* for *coxit, nun* for *non,* but *hoc* for *huc.* The character of this Latin is strange enough when written and must have been still more so when spoken: here is a specimen from so advanced a place as Viminacium: '*Lupus anemola ic avetat. Quot comidi mecum aveo. Ego Maurentia in hunc monumentum titulum posui Lupo virginio meo, cum quem quinquaginta annis bene laboravi adque inculpatim covixi; et Argenteo Samarconi (?) fratris vel subulele matris meae ipsum titulum feci*'.

To sum up: the Roman culture of Moesia Superior was neither old nor deep, but it grew stronger and more tenacious as Moesia and Dardania became the centre of the Empire and Naissus its capital. The Thraco-Illyrians of that region were slow to drop their native ways, but like the Getae of Moesia Inferior (as will be seen) they preserved their new civilizationwell.

In Pannonia the case was different. Here, once

Rome had decided to make the Danube her frontier and to use the Save valley as a great artery for communication with the East, she proceeded to organize municipal life in the new province without delay. First, she made sure of the great route which through Poetovio and Savaria led on to the Danube at Vindobona and Carnuntum, passing by a famous centre of Celtic civilization of the First and Second Iron Age, Scarbantia. Under Claudius Celeia became a *municipium* and Savaria a *colonia*: under the Flavian emperors, Siscia (which as we saw Augustus regarded as a possible headquarters for his Dacian offensive), and Sirmium became colonies, while Noviodunum, on the road to Siscia, and Scarbantia, on the road to Carnuntum, were raised to be *municipia*. But Romanization was carried out with equal effect on the outskirts of Pannonia and Noricum as well as on the great routes. Towns such as Celeia, Juvavum, Teurnia and Virunum became *municipia* under Claudius, and Solva received that privilege from the Flavians. Rhaetia, on the other hand, made no progress and remained, like Moesia Superior, in a half barbarous condition.

But a study of the monuments teaches us more still. The Roman culture of Noricum and of Pannonia was simply an extension and continuation of the life of Italy. So intense and prosperous was this culture in Cisalpine Gaul even in the first century that it became the deciding factor in the economic and political development of all Western and Central Europe. Once again a great Celtic unity, crossing Northern Italy, made its appearance in Europe, but this time Rome was the gainer. From Lugdunum in Gaul to Sirmium near the mouth of the Theiss, we see one world making use of one great line of communication upon which all other highways, whether from the Celtic Rhine or Danube, or from Latin Italy, converge. Every country traversed by this mighty route flourished the more because it shared in the prosperity of the whole.

It is worth our while examining more closely the form which Romanization took in these Illyrian and Celtic lands. In Dalmatia, in spite of its great length, the coast alone was important: the hinterland, the home of shepherds and woodmen (*fabri tignuarii*) and of the Illyrian miners was more like Moesia both in its rough poverty and in the scanty development of its urban life. The peasantry, of almost pure Illyrian stock, made admirable recruits: slow and heavy in mien, but obstinate and fierce fighters, they offered superb material for guarding the frontiers. But the towns of the coast-line, with Salonae at their head, were almost a part of Italy itself; for generations they had been enjoying the same type of culture and life, and their Latin was excellent, despite the mixture of races (Illyrian, Italian, Greek) to be found there. Naturally the most keen and lively elements in the interior of the country were drawn by these towns towards Italy; the Illyrian migrations of proto-historic times went on even into the first century A.D. and filled Italy with this fresh, vigorous, and hard-working stock.

The Roman culture of Pannonia presents quite a different aspect. No proper frontier exists between Italy and the Illyrian countries: where the Adriatic ends (and the sea is a link, not a barrier) the mountains begin. But in this region the Alps have a less rugged outline, and they resemble more a high plateau, dry and stony towards the sea, but with fair timber and pasture facing inland. The passes from Venetia into Pannonia do not present much difficulty, and once in the valley of the Save the traveller is well rewarded for the effort made; a rich and beautiful country extends from here right to the Danube, and the Romans when they were firmly set in Venetia could not fail to advance eastwards.

It was therefore only natural that this extension of Italy towards the east—with Aquileia for its base of operations—should have been officially recognized, even before the battle of Actium, by the first of the emperors. The campaigns of Octavian in 35 and 34 B.C. led to the foundation of several Roman towns, Tergeste (Trieste) and Pola on the Italian and Emona (Laibach) on the Illyrian side of the mountains. Siscia and Sirmium too began to play an important part and the whole valley of the Save was soon annexed. But Roman officialdom did not regard the newly won territory as secure and civilization did not at once take root with the legions on the Save and still less on the Danube; the constant revolts of the population down to the end of the reign of Augustus afford some justification for this cautious policy.

Yet, in spite of the insecurity and the risks, there were always peaceful pioneers of civilization who did not flinch from their task. It is interesting, for example, to note in the inscriptions of the upper valley of the Save how the civilian predominate over the military and how many purely native names appear in them. Here indeed we find a real Roman civilization created not by official decrees but through human activity working along natural economic lines: here the natives themselves renounced their nationality, took up Roman culture, and made it a thing of their own, to which Roman settlers could add little of importance. We can even watch Italian rites and beliefs moving eastward: in the territory of Emona we find the Italian festival of the *Rosalia*, celebrated by a guild of workmen (*fabri*) organized in *decuriae*, held in the same circumstances, the same month (June), and with the same ceremonies as in Italy. Along the great north-eastern route (the Amber Route of the prehistoric ages leading from the Adriatic, by Emona, Poetovio, Savaria, and Scarbantia to the Danube, then through Bohemia, and down the Elbe and the Vistula valleys), we find Romans travelling and trading, and filling with settlers and merchants such regions as the valley of the Arrabo, between Savaria and lake Pelso (Balaton), which had remained deserted ever since the victorious advance of Burebista had swept the Taurisci and Boii out of this territory. Thanks to the growth and prosperity of these civil farming settlements, due to individual initiative, and to the rapid commercial and industrial development of the district, a town such as Savaria became (as we have seen) a colony as early as the reign of Claudius, while Poetovio on the Drave, in spite of its more sheltered position, had to wait for this honour till the time of Trajan, and had afterwards to be reinforced by a military colony, simply because the pioneers of free settlement had passed it by. We have evidence of their presence even as far north as Bregetio, where inscriptions reveal the fact that the *Rosalia* began to be celebrated there.

Indeed, though the veterans when they settled down in civil life brought various rites and cults with them, these were usually foreign and oriental—their favourite gods are *Sol Invictus Mithras* or *Juppiter Dolichenus*, military gods *par excellence*—the civil settlers from Italy, whether farmers or business-men, brought and spread the old Italian cults such as those of *Liber Pater, Hercules, Silvanus, Fors Fortuna* (Nemesis), *Terra Mater* or *Diana*. It is therefore easy to distinguish between the Roman life of Pannonia Superior and of Noricum, civil and Italian in its origin, and that of Pannonia Inferior and of the frontier generally, which was military in its origin and cosmopolitan in its spirit: less Italian because more official. Just as in the valley of the Save we meet with *Aelii Carni cives Romani* of the Municipium Flavium Noviodunum, so we find large numbers of romanized natives on the great route towards Savaria and Scarbantia, and near Bregetio and Aquincum. *Collegia iuventutis*, as at Poetovio (with *praefecti* and *quinquennales*), or as at Adiaum (with a *magister*) must have existed in every town.

The great mass of the people bore Celtic names, which shows the importance of this element not only in Noricum but also in Pannonia, where the Illyrians were the earlier possessors. But there was no lack of support from the Celtic West. Treveri are found at Savaria, at Gerulata, at Carnuntum, etc., and Remi and Rhaeti elsewhere. Naturally enough on the Eastern Danube the Celtic element appears in strength, as for example in Pannonia Inferior, where the Eravisci to the north towards Aquincum and the Scordisci to the south towards Mursa, played an important part even under the Empire. Finally, there are the Celts of the East, e.g. the Cotini in Slovakia, who were destined to be received into the Empire and given land as a *civitas* in Celticized Pannonia.

Of one thing we may be sure, and that is that the introduction of agriculture into Eastern Pannonia by the Romans was extremely important: the emperors always regarded the settlement of Latin-speaking peasants upon the soil as an essential preliminary to any serious policy of Romanization. Yet, persistent and earnest as this agricultural life was, inscriptions about it are very few. We hear of *vicani Basoretanses* (somewhere towards the Danube), of *possessores vici Vindoniani* (not far from Aquincum), of a *villa Gai* (east of Vienna, in the *Itinerarium*), but that is all, so far as place-names can help us. There were, however, many veterans who had been settled in rural territory: and here it should be pointed out that the rural *territorium* of a town which was originally military, the *ager colonicus*, is quite a different thing from the *territorium legionis*, as for example at Aquincum. The community of veterans at Aquincum was a flourishing one: the magistrates of the municipality (later a colony) also possessed estates on which they erected fine buildings and tombs with lengthy screeds in verse. Yet, even so, the Celts were numerous and kept their standing much as it was before the arrival of the Romans. Aquincum had been founded *in territorio civitatis Eraviscorum*: now these Eravisci were a definite people who had once had their own king and their own coinage, samples of which have been found in Dacia (see Chap. IV, p. 137), and they must have been closely connected by routes across the plain of the Jazyges with the valley of the Mureş. This connection was preserved by the Romans, for the Roman road along the Mureş (Marisia) down to its confluence with the Theiss is well known, while for the bridgeheads of Trans Aquincum and Trans Bononiam erected '*in barbarico*' we have ample documentary evidence.

For, in spite of all dangers, commerce along

these frontiers with the wealthy and unsophisticated barbarians proved extremely profitable. To the north in the land of the Quadi, or to the east in the land of the Sarmatae, we find many traces of business men and merchants associated together in rich and influential guilds. At Mursa a *decurio coloniae, ob honorem flaminatus, tabernas L cum porticibus duplicibus in quibus mercatus ageretur pecunia sua fecit.* At Bregetio we find monuments dedicated *Genio commerci et negotiantum*: on the other side of the river, opposite Gran, in barbarian territory, arises, in 371 A.D., a *burgus, cui nomen Commercium* (these bridgeheads are in any case legion under the later Empire): at Trans Aquincum a *beneficiarius consularis*, the head of the imperial post station there, erects an altar *Genio commercii.* Scarbantia, which was a great junction for the roads of Northern Pannonia, was full of *negotiatores*; side by side with romanized Celts we find men from Salonae, and merchants from Aquileia at Annamatia.

It is obvious that after a century of military occupation (between 100 and 200 A.D.) Pannonia had become profoundly Roman: the soldiers married during their term of service and introduced the spirit of loyalty to the Empire into their families too. For instance, the dedication of a temple to *Nemesis* at Aquincum on the 24th

June (the exact date of the old Italian festival of Fors Fortuna) shows how genuine was the Roman culture that was spreading. School completed what the army could not do: Vergil was learnt by heart, and this training enabled a poet of Sirmium to express himself with ease and purity in Latin; these literary exercises, some of them addressed to the *dominus magister* (as were probably the moralizing verses found at Savaria), are not without an interest of their own.

Another instance can be found in the rural community of veterans settled at Aquae Iasae near lake Pelso. It gained such importance that after a disastrous fire it was completely restored by Constantine '*cum porticibus et omnibus orna-mentis ad pristinam faciem*', in order to enable it to hold its fairs regularly: '*nundinas die Solis perpeti*'. The literary evidence and the traditions which tell of the rapid development and of the opulence of the Christian church in Pannonia in the fourth and fifth centuries can also help us to realize how deeply civilization had driven its roots.

Yet there was a serious defect in this structure: it had no one powerful native people at its base. Celts there were in plenty, but so there were Illyrians, and Southern Thracians, and even Dacians (as soldiers). In addition there were

innumerable Syrians, and many Orientals—
Bithynians, Cappadocians, Greeks and Jews—
and even Berbers (*Mauri gentiles*) and Spaniards,
all these either stationed in the country as soldiers
or lured by the hope of commercial gain. And
this strange and confused congeries of nations,
with a mental outlook as varied and different as
the countries from which it was drawn, organized
though it was by Italians and penetrated with
their civilization, lived in constant terror of the
barbarians beyond the Danube. As early as 185,
Commodus '*ripam omnem burgis a solo extructis
item praesidiis per loca opportuna ad clandestinos
latrunculorum transitus oppositis munivit*', and
the story repeats itself ad infinitum down to the
close of the fourth century and even later. The
Roman life of Pannonia, real and powerful as it
was, being a direct continuation of that of North
Italy, did useful work and contributed towards
the Romanization of the Illyro-Thracians, but
after that, for lack of a sufficiently large local
ethnic base, it was doomed to be overwhelmed
by the Slav and Turanian barbarians.

Let us now examine the position on the Lower
Danube, in Moesia Inferior and in its southern
annex, Thrace. Here, in striking contrast with
Pannonia, we find on the arrival of the Romans
one great nation, the Thracian, dominating the

country: the southern branch of this great people were already penetrated with Hellenistic culture, but north of the Balkans the Daco-Getae of Moesia and Dacia had been won over to a more western type, which had been brought in by the Celts.

Apparently the despatch of Getic wheat to Rome by Plautius Silvanus in 52–53 A.D. produced a great impression of the fertility of Moesia: certainly, the number of settlers who flocked there to occupy the land and found estates (*villae*) all over the country, in friendly relations with the natives, from the time when Thracia down to the mouth of the Danube became a Roman province, was, as we shall see, extraordinarily large.

But before discussing this, we must make plain the position of the Thracians south of the Balkans. Like the Illyrians of Dalmatia, they were not an agricultural people (save in the valley of the Hebrus) but a race of shepherds, horse-breeders, and miners. For generations their kings had modelled themselves upon the partially hellenized monarchies they saw around them in Scythia or Asia Minor, and so had succeeded more or less in hellenizing themselves and their subjects. When the Romans occupied Macedonia they were faced for long years with warfare against their eastern neighbour, and only towards the close of the first century B.C. did they succeed in taming and turning them into independent but serviceable allies against the other barbarians. When the emperor Claudius, irritated by the unceasing civil wars of the petty Thracian princes, finally decided to make the country into a province, he had no intention of transforming it into a romanized district: he simply contented himself with doing what his predecessors had consistently done before him—in spite of bloody revolts, as in the time of Tiberius—that is, recruiting for infantry and cavalry in the largest possible numbers from these unconquerable tribes, whose greatest joy was to sport with death, if not on the field of battle, at any rate in the amphitheatre. For this reason Thracia received an organization all its own, upon Hellenistic lines, and the Greek language and customs were sedulously protected by the Romans, who were quite ready to regard this province as making part of the Hellenic half of the Empire. In Rome, in Italy, and throughout the Empire, Thracian recruits and Thracian troops are frequently met. Naturally they became romanized and soon merged with the population of the other provinces, while Thrace, which rarely saw her sons return to her, dwindled away into complete insignificance, a country of primitive culture, whose only task—practically—was to furnish first to the Greek world and later to the hellenized Empire of the East rough but valuable human material, used by its masters regardless of life or cost.

Very different was the state of affairs north of the Balkans. Like Herodotus, five centuries before, the Romans under Claudius had grasped the fact that another world began here. It was the home of the Getae (of whom the Moesi formed a part), a nation which stretched as far north as Moravia, Silesia, Galicia, and the Ukraine. From long time past they had been tillers of the soil. Greek respect for these early disciples of Demeter was symbolized in the legend that represented the Getic king Charnabon as a worshipper of Triptolemus; successive waves of invasion (Iranian, Celtic, and Germanic, in Moldavia and Wallachia or in Bulgaria and the Dobruja) had not turned this settled and persistent people from its task. Ovid tells us that the Getae of his time guided the plough with one hand and kept the other on their sword to protect themselves against the wild horsemen from beyond the Danube. Nomads were their natural enemies, but agriculturalists who came among them were counted as friends. Apart from the Romans one people, the Bessi, proved to be the inseparable companion

of the Getae of the Lower Danube. The punitive
expeditions of M. Lucullus in 72 and of Crassus
in 29 B.C. against the Thracians of the Rhodope
region had resulted in a strong movement of
emigration among these Bessi to the north-east,
beyond the Balkan mountains, which did not
stop till they had reached Scythia Minor. Here
they made common cause with the Getae and on
the entry of the Romans into this region *Bessi
consistentes* were to be found on every side. They
got on equally well with the Roman farmers,
and throughout the land, in the *territoria* of the
Getae, there arose *vici* of *cives Romani et Bessi
consistentes*, in which the *magistri* and *quaestores*
were elected every year by friendly consent from
each nation alternately, or, if there were two
places to fill, a *Romanus* and a *Bessus* would sit
side by side.

Finally in 46 A.D. Claudius extended the Roman
frontier of the Danube right down to the Black
Sea: he saw to the organization of the customs
service, and delimited the rural territories of the
Greek cities on the coast, of the auxiliary *castella*
on the Danube, and of the native *civitates*; but
most important of all was the wise step he took
in cutting off the so-called *ripa Thraciae* (which
was completely peopled by the Getae, and comprised the eastern half of what was later known as

Moesia Inferior, between the river Asamus and
the Euxine), from the province of Thracia and
including it in the Danubian provinces which
were under the Roman system of organization
and administration.

It is interesting to note that this refashioning
of territory in the Danubian basin had already
had a precedent on the other side of the river
under Augustus. In the interval between the
two Pannonian revolts (and therefore at some
time before 6 A.D.) a legate of Augustus not only
inflicted a severe defeat on the Dacians in their
own country, '*tribus eorum ducibus cum magna
copia caesis*', but also transplanted 50,000
Dacians into Moesia, settling them to the south
of the Danube. It seems likely, furthermore, that
a broad strip of territory north of the river as far
as the 'little Roman vallum' in Wallachia (between Calafat and Giurgiu) was then incorporated
into the Empire as a sort of extended bridgehead
to face Ratiaria, Oescus, and Novae. Fifty years
later, 52–53 A.D., Plautius Silvanus made his
great demonstration of Roman might down the
whole course of the Danube to the sea-coast, and
sent embassies with demands or threats, as far
as the Crimea: Tyras came under Roman rule,
and Olbia and Chersonesus accepted with gratitude the protection that Rome offered them—a

generous offer, for she did not impose her suzerainty over them as yet. In any case the great Moldo-Wallachian plain was thoroughly pacified, first by the establishment of a whole series of small client-kingdoms, from which Silvanus took hostages for greater security, and second (as the epitaph of the great governor expressly says), 'by enlarging the frontiers of the province'; this can only mean on the left bank of the Danube, and the enlargement probably extended to the 'great Roman vallum' in Wallachia and the southerly vallums in Moldavia and Bessarabia. One hundred thousand *Transdanuviani* were also settled in Moesia.

Some years later Vespasian reorganized the Danube flotilla—which had already done good service since 15 A.D. under the command of the governor (or in his absence under the *praefectus orae maritimae*) and gave it a new name, *Classis Flavia Moesica*. At the same time he assigned to it bases lower down the river, each with its respective camp, buildings, and rural territory, such as every body of troops stationed on the frontier possessed.

Between the death of Augustus and that of Claudius (14–54 A.D.), within less than fifty years, all that vast expanse of territory between the Danube and the Balkans, from the frontier of

modern Yugo-Slavia to the Roumanian coast
of the Black Sea (that is to say, all Northern
Bulgaria and the Dobruja) had been conquered,
refashioned, and reorganized by the splendid
generals whom Rome had sent out, nominally
to be no more than governors of (the later) Moesia
Superior. But they had completely grasped the
high mission entrusted to them along the whole
of the Lower Danube and the Thracian coast of
the Black Sea. In 54 A.D., at latest, we find
Tullius Geminus, the *legatus pro praetore* of
Claudius, receiving at Tomi a deputation of ten
citizens from Istria, who had come to beg him to
confirm their ancient rights over their rural
territory and their privilege of free fishing in the
Danube. The presence of the governor of Moesia
at Tomi cannot be due to accident: rather we are
forced to believe that Flavius Sabinus must, after
46 A.D., have introduced the custom of residing
officially for some time at Tomi in order to exercise a general supervision over those matters
which came within the competence of the *praefectus orae maritimae*. Indeed, the correspondence
discovered at Istria lays such weight on the
decisions of Sabinus and on the friendliness he
evinced to the Greeks, while the orders that
Sabinus must have given with regard to the
ὁροθεσία of all the cities on the Pontic coast,

rendered his presence on the spot so desirable that it seems necessary to assign a very important part in the Romanization of the province to this Flavius. The effect of his beneficent rule on Moesia must have been very great, and we should possibly ascribe some part of the large number of *Flavii* (the new Roman citizens in the coast towns or in the inland Romano-Thracian villages) to his patronage, and not to that of his brother Vespasian, who did not become emperor till twenty years later.

Moreover it must be realized that this Romanization cannot have been due to any legionary settlements, for camps along the Lower Danube east of the Olt did not exist till after the death of Nero. Then, in order to guard the mouth of this important valley which offered so easy a path to invaders from Transylvania, Vespasian planted the *Legio V Macedonica* at Oescus, and his son Domitian settled the *Legio I Italica* at Novae. Trajan was the first to place legions further East: he established the *Legio XI Claudia* at Durostorum and the *Legio V Macedonica* at Troesmis, while Oescus was raised to the proud rank of Colonia Ulpia. Therefore until his reign, there can be no question of any save auxiliary troops acting as garrison for the greater part of Moesia Inferior. Now these troops cannot have counted for much as an actual romanizing element, since they stood in need of it themselves, nor is the question of their settlement in *castella* built along the bank of the river relevant here, since it did not take place, along the Lower Danube, till after the reign of Trajan.

Yet, by the beginning of the second century, Moesia was already thoroughly romanized: the inscriptions of this period give us evidence for a Roman tradition which was already old. Roman civilians, with the gentile names of Flavius (after the four Flavians, Sabinus, Vespasian, Titus, and Domitian) or of Cocceius (after Nerva) are to be found in numbers not only in the Greek cities and their rural territory, but in the Romano-Thracian *vici*, *pagi*, and *territoria* as well. The Italian festival of the *Rosalia* is found here, as well as in Pannonia, celebrated by the peasants, and it has even become the great yearly festival at which the *magistri* and *quaestores* of the *vici* consecrate votive altars to the supreme god *Iuppiter Optimus Maximus* on behalf of the safety and prosperity of the imperial family.

This cannot be due, as we have seen, to any military occupation: the explanation lies in the fact that the Danube, with its tributary the Save, had once again done its duty as a highway be-

tween the Adriatic and the Black Sea: a current
of colonization set in towards the lands of the
Lower Danube and drew with it genuine Roman
elements from Italy, from Noricum, from Dalmatia, and from Pannonia. These men bought
parcels of land, sometimes together, sometimes
singly—we can see them *ad villam suam* in some
pagus or *territorium*—and gradually they helped
to found whole *vici* which grew up around their
praedia and their *villae*, and these villages
naturally took the name of their founder—*vicus
Clementiani, vicus Quintionis, vicus Secundini,
vicus Celeris*, and so on.

Consequently, when veterans themselves began
to settle there, after Domitian and Trajan, so
great was the pressure of things Roman throughout the whole country that not only the rural
territories of the Greek cities, but even the Greek
cities themselves began to be romanized, accept-
ing Latin feasts (*Rosalia*) and the Latin language.
In proof of this we can cite two instances which
are extremely significant. Trajan, out of his
respect for the Hellenism of Thrace, thought it
his duty to found cities of a Greek type in Moesia
Inferior too—Marcianopolis (to the east of
Odessus) and Nicopolis ad Istrum (to the south
of Novae). Neither the one nor the other succeeded for a moment in stemming the Roman

tide: on the contrary, it is precisely Nicopolis
that has preserved for us an extremely interesting
list of names of the *Bacchium vernaculorum*: in
this *album* we can remark once more how
Thracians, Romans, and Greek-speaking Orientals
have all alike been caught up by the wave of
western influence.* Furthermore, and the fact is
worth emphasizing, this is no superficial veneer
of culture, where names may change but the substance remain unaltered as in the case of the
innumerable Syrians, Egyptians, or Greeks, who
adopted good old Roman names but retained
unchanged their language, their customs, and
their mentality. Here we are brought face to
face (as in the West) with free and willing collaboration, a mutual give-and-take: here we have
the spectacle of the native who continues to call
himself *Glagissa Glagissae filius*, *Ithazis Dada*, or
Burtzitzinis, to worship his Thracian deities, to
reside in *vici* or *civitates* of Thracian name and
Thracian organization (such as *Scenopesis* or
Ausdecensis), and yet who is more and more
proud of being a citizen of the Empire, of speaking
Latin, and of representing, together with the
vernaculi of the region, the traditions of that

---

* It is worthy of observation that Getic names such as
Decebalus and *Burobusta* occur on this list, as in the similar
inscription of Durostorum.

local culture which was yearly driving its roots deeper.

It is only natural, then, that all the Orientals whom business brought into Moesia and profit urged to settle there should give up their 'Asianism', cease speaking Greek, and adopt the Roman forms of life. Similarly the merchants and the functionaries of the imperial departments, especially of the customs—the revenues of which from the rich plains of what are now Roumania and Russia must have been considerable—men of urban and sometimes servile origin, cosmopolitan as they were, felt themselves forced to help in the work of Romanization too, because the greater part of the people lived on the land and all this large farming population (*pagani*) had become Roman.

The god *par excellence* of all these peasants and farmers is *Silvanus*: here, as in Italy and the West, he is *sanctus, domesticus, silvester*, but here also he is *Sanctus Silvanus Sator*. In this form he appears for the first time at Ulmetum in the *territorium Capidavense*, both in an image sculptured upon the tombstone of the *princeps loci, C. Julius C. f. Quadratus* (towards the beginning of the second century), and also in a dedication of an altar by the *consacrani* on the 1st June, 178 (probably on the occasion of the great yearly feast of the *Rosalia*) in which the *cives Romani et Bessi consistentes vico Ulmeto* took part.

Upon this sure foundation, sure both economically and socially, the city life of Moesia developed to a remarkable degree. Oescus, Colonia Ulpia, Ulpia Nicopolis (ad Istrum), Durostorum (municipium Aurelium), Troesmis, Municipium Montanensium Marcianopolis, Abrittus, Tropaeum Traiani, all these towns bear witness to a creative effort in the realm of commerce, industry and art which would not have shamed centres and provinces far more sheltered from invasion than Moesia could ever be. When we consider that the gloomy tale of disaster begins as early as the reign of Marcus Aurelius with a great raid of the Daci Costoboci, we must admit that this culture evinced a remarkable tenacity. Two centuries later when Christian missionaries visited the province, they found it a rich and prosperous region, and even as late as the year 600 Byzantine generals on their expeditions towards the Danube were to find Latin-speaking peasants still toiling in the fields, while in the towns, ruled by bishops, the spirit of affection and loyalty towards Rome remained unshaken.

Finally, we must consider what was the position of affairs which Trajan found in Dacia when he took the momentous decision of incorporating it as a province of the Empire.

First of all, Dacia was a great kingdom based upon a solid and homogeneous ethnic foundation: its historical traditions were already old, its social and economic structure was well marked, and it possessed an advanced culture, which, influenced at first by the forms of Celtic civilization, had for two centuries before Trajan felt the impress of the Roman. Here was a worthy rival even for Rome. This was no mere agglomeration of a number of savage tribes with a shifting population, scattered loosely over an extended territory, with a complete lack of political and national cohesion, such as Rome had found in Dalmatia or Thrace or Pannonia or Moesia; here was a nation, organized, powerful, conscious of itself. Indeed, the Dacians, as a nation, never accepted Roman rule: those who had not fallen in the two great wars withdrew sullenly into Northern Dacia, a land untouched by Roman conquest, and from there, either by themselves or in company with migrating bodies of Germans, made continual raids upon the province, as 'free Dacians', until in the end the Romans under Aurelian retired to the right bank of the river and left Dacia in the hands of the Goths. It is this exodus of the Dacians to the free north that accounts for the very restricted number of Dacian *auxilia* to be found in the Roman imperial armies. We can only trace one *ala* (raised by Trajan himself), and but four or five *cohortes* (raised either by Trajan or his successor), while peoples far less numerous than the Dacians, such as, for instance, the Thracians and the Dalmatians (not to mention the Syrians or Spaniards) contributed a very considerable number of auxiliary troops.

Owing to the desperate resistance offered by the native population, Trajan gave the province an organization of a very peculiar character. In the first place he had resort to forced colonization, and invited or compelled a very large number of romanized provincials to come and settle in the new territory: the salt mines and gold mines of the country, for instance, were worked and developed by men with special technical knowledge, the Pirustae, who were brought from Dalmatia. But in addition he drew the frontiers of the province in such a way that the two great plains over which the mountain massif of Dacia towers (the Moldo-Wallachian steppe in the east, and the plain of the Theiss and its tributaries in the west), remained entirely outside its limits: he appears to have regarded the aim of the province as being simply, like a fortress, to hold the mountain region in subjection.

It was a short-sighted policy, and as a result the position soon became untenable. Marcus Aurelius found himself compelled to allow the Sarmatians of the Hungarian plain (the Jazyges) to pass through Roman Dacia on their way to visit their kinsmen in Bessarabia and the Ukraine, a measure which anticipated by one hundred years the withdrawal from the province. And although this very emperor made three provinces of the two Daciae which Hadrian had established, it was an apparent increase only, for they never comprised anything more than the mountain regions. The Romans had a strange horror of the desert, and consequently of the boundless steppe plains which resembled them; they dealt with the nomads of the two great plains of Dacia and Pannonia exactly as they had with the nomads of the Sahara. Special troops, Syrians, archers of the eastern desert, were garrisoned here, as in Africa, to police the two 'deserts' on the east and the west of the Dacian provinces. And that was all.

But this is true only from the official standpoint: real life has its own rules and practice based on a common sense very different from the artificial regulations of the politicians. If the average Roman merchant or ordinary citizen, staying at Bregetio or Aquincum, or even at Intercisa or

Vetus Salina, found that personal business called him to Dacia, it was absurd to suppose that he would make an immense semi-circular journey through Singidunum and Viminacium in order to reach Sarmizegetusa, Apulum, Napoca, or Porolissum. Instead of such a waste of time he chose a simpler and more direct route, for the Sarmatians of the Hungarian plain had no interest (save in wartime) in hindering free travel between Pannonia Inferior and Dacia through their territory. They stood to gain greatly from it, and in any case they were more or less client-subjects of Rome. The position is illustrated even more clearly in Moldavia. The Romans never occupied it officially: yet it was Trajan himself who fortified a camp at Bărboşi, near the mouth of the Seret (where the Greeks of the sixth century B.C. had once had an ἐμπόριον) and established auxiliary troops there, together with a detachment from the *classis Flavia Moesica*, whose business it was to police the waters of the Hierasus (Seret). Around Bărboşi numerous settlers and farmers formed a *territorium*, and we actually know the name of one of its *quinquennales*, *L. Julius Julianus, qui et Rundacio* (the native name Ῥυνδάκης). There was even a Roman road, connecting the towns of Scythia Minor directly with Eastern Dacia, which started from Bărboşi (which would draw the traffic from Dinogetia and from Troesmis), led up the Hierasus past the Romano-Dacian *vici* of Sendreni and Poiana, and then turning up the valley of the Trotuş towards the Oituz Pass finally reached the Roman Camp of Breţcu in South-eastern Transylvania. But there was, besides, a route from Olbia, which led past Tyras and through Bessarabia and Moldavia, directly into Transylvania, that is, through the regions occupied by the Eastern Sarmatians (the Roxolani), who were themselves client-subjects of Rome, and who had frequent complaints to make (as, for instance, in the year after Trajan's death, to Hadrian *de imminutis stipendiis*). This road appears to have been not only much used, but also officially recognized, for the Ravenna Geographer enumerates its stations.

This unofficial 'Dacia' then, as contrasted with the official provinces, bordered on Pannonia Inferior in the west and on those regions in the east between the Pyretus and the Bosporus where the Romans had a sort of protectorate over the Geto-Iranian peoples. Two districts of this 'Dacia' bore a great resemblance to Moesia, the Banat and Oltenia (Little Wallachia): they had never opposed the same stubborn resistance to Rome as the mountaineers, and apparently after the first Dacian War they made their peace with her; the inhabitants of these large and fertile territories resigned themselves easily to the new system and were rapidly romanized. This is certainly true of such a region of Little Wallachia as the lower valley of the Alutus: here we encounter a rural organization of the natives into *territoria*, with a council of *curiales*, grouped around an old stronghold like Sucidava: here too are to be found wealthy native landholders, who have become completely romanized, such as *Esbenus*, for instance, who hails from the *territorium Sucidavense*, and whose official name is *Ael(ius) Vale(n)s*. Like every rich Roman he had a great household of slaves, and we still possess the funeral monument which they raised in his honour to show the gratitude they felt for their manumission.

Like Pannonia Inferior, Dacia, being a frontier province studded with camps (there were two legions stationed there and a number of auxiliary troops), was bound to be colonized also by the veterans, who soon gained the predominance over the civil settlers. The natural riches of this fine country offered these retired soldiers admirable opportunities for settling down and making a home, and as most of them married native wives during their term of service (starting from the second century), small centres of Roman culture grew up around the numerous camps and fortresses, *villae, vici, pagi, regiones*.* Even a large city such as Apulum took its origin from the *canabae* of the XIIIth legion.

But in any event the commerce and traffic that a land so richly endowed by nature was bound to stimulate, attracted to the country a crowd of business men and agents of all nations, Treverans, Asiatics, and Galatians. It was not merely from some small fair or group of huts around a camp that most of the cities sprang up; towns such as Drobeta, Tsierna, Romula and Napoca rose and flourished, thanks to their active business and commerce, while such places as Germisara or Ad Mediam owed their prosperity to their fame as watering places and health resorts. The *negotiatores*, organized in *collegia* according to the different provinces (we know those of Dacia Apulensis), with their *defensores*, could not only dispatch their wares and products by roads and land routes, but were able to make use of the great rivers of Dacia as well, for inscriptions reveal several *collegia* of *utricularii*, just as in Gaul. Dedications to the *Genius Commerci*, such as we

* It is interesting to note that Roumanian alone among the Romance languages has kept the word *veteranus*, in the form '*bătrân*', to express the idea of 'old'.

have already met in Pannonia, were made by the
officials of the customs service, as, for instance, at
Micia on the Lower Mureş, where the mountains
of Transylvania sink down into the Hungarian
plain: *Iovi optimo maximo terrae Daciae et Genio
populi Romani et commerci*. This active inland
business life was balanced by commercial expansion abroad, which took merchants and wares
from Dacia as far as Salonae, or Mitylene, or even
into Egypt.

If we bear in mind this vast new territory, rich
in gold and mineral wealth, with its large estates
(belonging to the emperors or in private owner-
ship) worked and exploited by an army of slaves
and freedmen, with imperial agents, civil and
military (there were three *procuratores* for the
three Dacias), with a large army and a corresponding number of veteran settlers, we can easily
understand that the Roman culture of Dacia was
more full and complete than any east of the Alps
and Adriatic, and—it must be confessed—the
most cosmopolitan too. At first sight the inscriptions seem to reveal a veritable chaos of
nationalities, religions, occupations, and interests,
but further analysis is possible, and careful
scrutiny soon reveals the difference between the
settled and working elements and the mere adventurers or agents of exploitation.

When in 270 the order was given to evacuate
Dacia, all the soldiers, imperial officials, and
business men left and the cities sank into decay.
But the peasants, on their little strips of land,
stayed behind, and they were by now, 150 years
after the conquest, extremely numerous. During
the continual wars waged by the Romans against
the 'free Dacians' of the north, many of these had
been colonized side by side with the veterans, as
had happened in the time of Aelius Catus and
Plautius Silvanus in Moesia; other Dacians too
from the lonely valleys among the mountains had
joined with them. But the basis of the country
population of Dacia in 270 remained that provided by the veterans who year by year for a
century and a half had settled down on Dacian
soil. In contrast with the two Moesiae, where
Triballi, Getae, and Bessi had been romanized
in large numbers, but for that very reason had
somewhat lowered the standard of culture, Dacia
stood out as far more Roman. If proof is needed
it is enough to take the scanty monuments of
rural Moesia with their naïve sculpture and decoration, and contrast them with the fine inscriptions and the wealth of monuments in Dacia.
A foreigner, who cannot grasp at once the purity
of the Latin still to be found in the Roumanian
language should bear in mind the facts adduced

in this chapter; they are based on literary and archaeological evidence, and on inscriptions which he can examine and verify. Consideration of these should save him from such curious hypotheses as a 'Balkan Romanism, Thraco-Illyrian rather than Roman', which some savants have seen fit to put forth.

The aim of this chapter has been to show the way in which Roman life and civilization established itself on the soil of Dacia, in forms as full and genuine as it had exhibited in Pannonia, Dalmatia, or even Northern Italy: yet, deep-rooted though it was, it must have been swept away in a few generations if it had been able to rely only upon its own resources. Fortunately, it did not: we have seen that a much larger 'Dacia' than the territory comprised within the three provinces, practically indeed the whole extent of the old empire of Burebista, had been under Roman influence. The success of the Roman colonizing effort was due to work that had been done long beforehand, and the seed fell on ground already prepared. It was due not only to the natural features and economic conditions of the Danube basin, but also to the movement of peoples and to successive waves of culture that had surged over that vast area during many generations.

The Danube basin has been from the earliest times (e.g. the Villanovan age in Chapter I) a world complete in itself. When the long struggle between Dacia and Rome was finally decided, Rome had already brought unity of civilization to that whole area: she gave much, but she received something back as well and from this inter-action a special type of civilization grew up, differing in some of its manifestations, though little in spirit, from the Roman culture of Gaul or Spain.

The Romans could never establish themselves properly in a country unless they introduced their own agricultural civilization. Now the Danube basin, ever since the Neolithic Age, has been an almost classic region for agriculture. But the agricultural civilization of Italy, and of the Empire generally, was almost identical materially with that of the Celts of the second Iron Age, and the migration of the Celtic peoples towards the Orient had by the fourth century B.C. imposed an uniform economic life over this whole area. Consequently the way was already paved for the Roman settlers and when they arrived they introduced, apart from the Latin language, practically nothing that was new to the natives. The industries of the late La Tène period, for instance, continued uninterrupted during the Roman occupation and even after their withdrawal.

Religious movements, Mithraism first, and Christianity later, in their turn helped to cement and build up this uniformity of culture. But the eastern forms of Christianity and the Greek-speaking missionaries, although they had displayed great activity in the Black Sea, the Aegean, and the Adriatic, failed to secure any hold here; the peasants would not accept Christianity save in its Latin form. The apostle of the Romano-Getic peoples (starting in the year 380) was a Latin, the bishop Nicetas of Remesiana, the friend of Paulinus of Nola. Even the apostle of the Goths, Ulfilas, found that he must preach in Latin to win the attention of this people. In modern Roumanian the principal terms of the Christian religion are of Latin origin, and even more Latin than in the other Romance languages (we have already observed a parallel case, on page 195): Italian and French derive their 'chiesa' and 'église' from ἐκκλησία, but Roumanian uses the word 'biserica', from the Latin *basilica*.

The Latin elements still to be found in the Danube region to-day do not owe their origin to a race of shepherds or miners, whether Illyrian or Thracian: they are derived directly from the old Danubian farming population, which extended from the western frontier of Pannonia Superior right down to the delta of the Danube.

It is the unity and extensiveness of this Romano-Danubian culture which offers the most satisfactory explanation of certain identical linguistic forms found in the Alps and the Carpathians. These elements preserved at their best precisely in the Dacia of Decebalus and within its boundaries cannot be of Balkan origin, for the very sufficient reason that the Balkans were never romanized. They are essentially and exclusively Danubian: their persistence during the severe trials of the Middle Ages and their ultimate survival were possible because all the romanized peoples of the Danube countries had lent their support. It is the high quality of that culture, which reached Pannonia and Moesia Inferior first, and Dalmatia and Moesia Superior immediately after, that has determined the essentially Latin characteristics of modern Roumanian life.

When the Slavonic invasions began, the pastoral life of Dalmatia and of Moesia Superior gradually gave way and disappeared. But the agricultural civilization of Dacia and of Moesia Inferior stood out and has survived down to our own day. Pannonia too fought well for the Latin cause since she also possessed this Roman agricultural life: recent discoveries seem to suggest that the struggle lasted down into the tenth century. But in the end the lack of territorial continuity with Dacia and Moesia proved fatal; isolated and thrown upon her own resources she fell a victim to the combined onslaught of Slavs, Magyars, and Germans. For this reason Roumania, instead of being a peninsula jutting out from a Latin mainland towards the east, has remained an island, a large island it is true, but cut off and far distant from the main body of her Latin kinsmen.

BIBLIOGRAPHICAL NOTE

The late Professor Pârvan had published the following contributions (books and articles) on questions falling within the scope of this volume.

1. *Getica, o Protoistorie a Daciei.* Bucarest, 1926.

   This volume contains a lengthy résumé in French, together with a wealth of bibliographical material and a very large number of illustrations.

2. *Inceputurile vietii Romane la gurile Dunării.* Bucarest, 1923.

   This deals mainly with the subject matter of chap. III of this volume and is in Roumanian only. It contains over a hundred illustrations. See also:

   I primordi della civiltà Romana alle foci del Danubio. (Ausonia: vol. x, 1921, pp. 198 *sqq.*)

   La pénétration hellénique et hellénistique dans la vallée du Danube. (Bull. Hist. Acad. Roum. x, 1923, pp. 43 *sqq.*)

   Nuove considerazioni sul vescovato della Scizia Minore. (Rendiconti Pontif. Accad. II, 1924; Rome.)

   Note di geografia antica. (Rivista di Filologia, LI, 1923, pp. 333 *sqq.*)

   Municipium Aurelium Durostorum. (Ibid. LII, 1924, pp. 3 *sqq.*)

3. *Archäologische Funde in Rumänien.* (Arch. Anzeiger, Jahrb. d. Deut. Arch. Inst., Berlin, 1913, 14 and 15.)

204   BIBLIOGRAPHICAL NOTE

4. In the Annals of the Roumanian Academy (*Analele Academiei Române*), Bucarest, Pârvan published the following articles:

Cetatea Tropaeum (1912).
Cetatea Ulmetum, I–IV (1912–14).
Descoperiri nouă in Scythia Minor (1913).
Ştiri nouă din Dacia Malvensis (1913).
Castrul dela Poiana şi Drumul Roman prin Moldova de jos (1913).
Zidul cetătii Tomi (1915).
Histria IV (1916).
Gerusia din Callatis (1919).
Consideratii asupra unor nume de râuri dacoscitice (1922).
Aşezări geto-grece şi daco-romane în câmpia munteană (1923).

5. The first two volumes of *Dacia—Recherches et Découvertes archéologiques en Roumanie*, of which he was the editor, also contain some contributions by Pârvan.

Vol. I.   *Une nouvelle inscription de Tomi* (pp. 273–9).
L'âge du dépôt de bronze de Suseni (pp. 359–62).
A propos du "basileus" Cotys (pp. 363–7).

Vol. II.   *Fouilles d'Histria* (pp. 198–248).
Un aes grave olbien à Salsovia (pp. 420–1).
La "statue-menhir" de Hamangia (pp. 422–9).

6. Mention should perhaps also be made of his *Contributionii epigrafici la Istoria Crestinismului daco-român.* (Bucarest, 1911; in Roumanian only.)

PLATE 1

1 and 4, Swan forms from Guşteriţa; 2, Bronze goblet from Madacska (Nograd); 3, Handle of a bronze vase from near Huniedoara; 5, Bronze goblet from Hajdú-Böszörmény; 6, Copper pot with three legs from the Braşov district; 7, *Situla* from Hajdú-Böszörmény; 8, Bronze cauldron from Hadjú-Böszörmény; 9, Votive car from Orăştie.

After Goos, *Skizzen*, *Archiv des Vereins für siebenbürgische Landeskunde*, XIII, 1876, p. 534.

PLATE 2

Convex gold disc from Otlaca, after Márton, *Arch. Ért.* XXIX, 1909, p. 408.

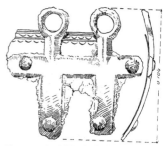

Fragment of North Italic cauldron from Alba Iulia (Brukenthal Museum, Sibiu).

Bronze cauldron from Máriapócs, after Josa, *Arch. Ért.* XXII, 1902, p. 278.

Bronze cauldron from Kántorjánosi.

PLATE 3

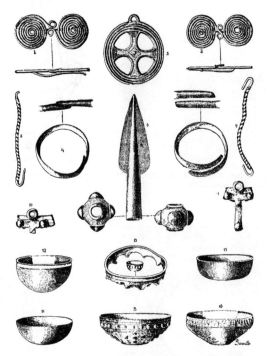

Bronze deposit from Fizeşul Gherlii, after Hampel,
Arch. Ért. xv, 1895, p. 199.

PLATE 4

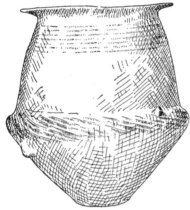

Clay vase from Târgul Mureşului, after
Kovács, *Dolgozatok*, VI, 1905, p. 248.

Italic bronze vase from Corneto,
after Kovács.

Terra cotta plaque from Sighişoara, after Petranu, *Muzeele din
Transilvania*, p. 149.

Stone plaque from Nesac-
tium, after Hoernes, *Mitt. d.
Zentr.-Komm.* II, 1, 1905,
p. 337.

PLATE 5

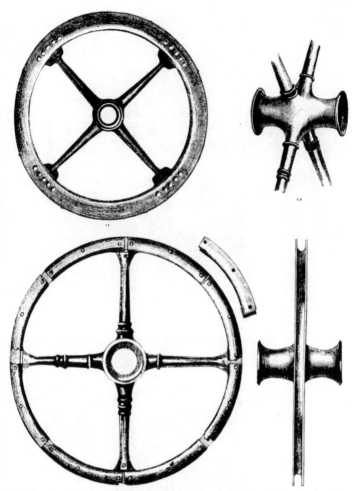

Wheels of a war chariot from Abos (above) and from Arcalia (below), after
Hampel, *Bronzkor*, I, pl. LIX.

PLATE 6

The hydria from Bene, after Pósta, *Dolgozatok*, v, 1914, p. 19; now at the Archaeological Museum of the University of Cluj.

Lower part of the vertical handle of the hydria from Bene, after Pósta, *Dolgozatok*, v, 1914, p. 22.

PLATE 7

Bronze figure of Anaïtis from Năeni
(front view).

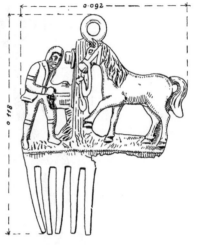

Scythian comb from Bucarest.

Scythian harness ornaments from Craiova, after Schuchhardt, *Alteuropa* (1919), p. 332.

PLATE 8

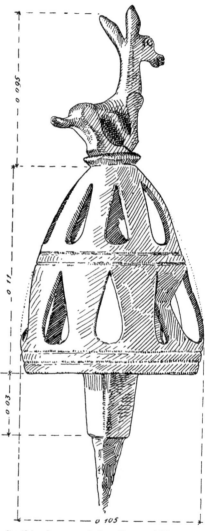

Scythian bronze pole-top, Bucarest Museum.

PLATE 9

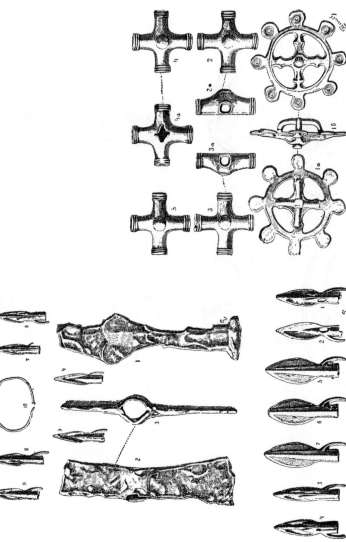

Hallstatt bronze ornaments (right) and Scythian remains (left) from Aiud, after Herepeĭ, *Arch. Ért.* XVII, 1897, pp. 64–5.

PLATE 10

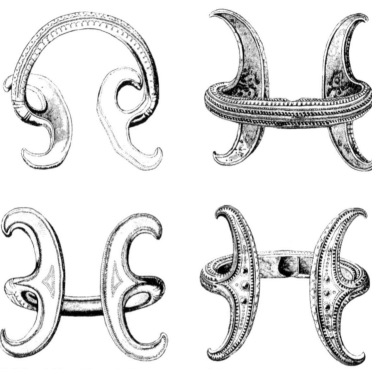

Gold bracelet from Pipea, after Hampel,
Arch. Ért. xiv, 1880, p. 215.

Gold bracelet from Biia, after Hampel,
Arch. Ért. xiv, 1880, p. 214.

PLATE 11

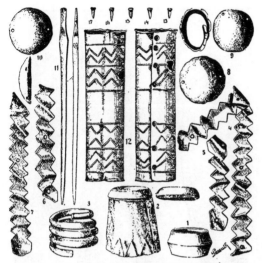

Gold treasure from Gyoma, after Márton, *Arch. Ért.* xxv, 1905, p. 236.

Gold fibula from Mikhalkovo, after Hadaczek, *Jahreshefte,* x, 1906, p. 35.

PLATE 12

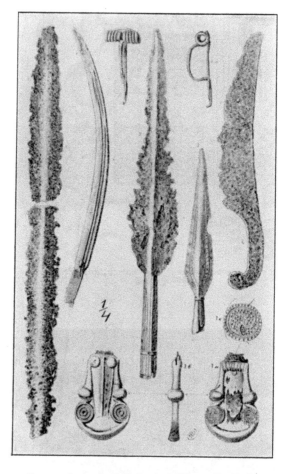

Some contents of a Celtic tomb at Silivaş, after Roska,
Archivele Olteniei, v, 1926, p. 50.

PLATE 13

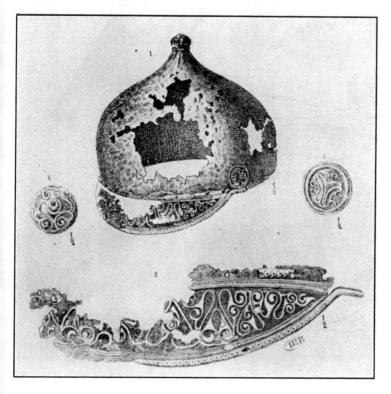

Above: Archaeo-La'Tène helmet from the county of Túrócz, after Reinecke, *Arch. Ért.*
XVIII, 1898, p. 311. Below: Helmet of Italic type, but of Celtic workmanship, from the
tomb at Silivas (after Roska).

PLATE 14

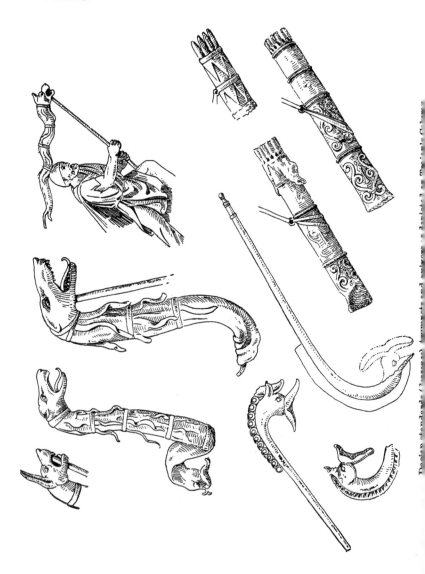

Prow ornaments (*tanema*), figureheads, and spears, as depicted on The icinic Galaxes.

PLATE 15

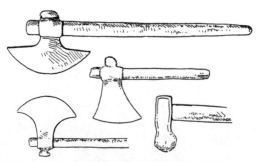

Types of Dacian battle-axe (*cateia*) as depicted on
Trajan's Column.

Stone alignment II at Costeşti.

PLATE 16

Stone circle at Grădiştea Muncelului.

INDEX AND CONCORDANCE
OF PLACE NAMES

In the text the names of all places lying within the present
frontiers of Roumania are given in their official Roumanian
form unless there is a recognized English equivalent. As,
however, many of the finds made in Transylvania were first
published by Hungarian archaeologists, the Magyar forms
have also been included for the more important of the places
in question. Where neither the Roumanian nor the Magyar
place-names are familiar to English readers, the German forms
have been added in so far as they exist. The modern equivalents
for classical place-names have also been given where they are
likely to be useful. In the following list italics are used to
denote ancient place-names; G. represents the German, M. the
Magyar, and *mod.* the modern equivalent of the form given in
the text. R. stands for river. All the place-names in this index
are shown on the map and an indication of the section where
they are to be found precedes the reference to the page number
in the text. The frontiers traced on the map itself are those of
the Danubian countries as they are to-day.

GENERAL INDEX

For EU product safety concerns, contact us at Calle de José Abascal, 56–1°,
28003 Madrid, Spain or eugpsr@cambridge.org.

www.ingramcontent.com/pod-product-compliance
Ingram Content Group UK Ltd.
Pitfield, Milton Keynes, MK11 3LW, UK
UKHW020318140625
459647UK00018B/1922